MW01125308

Baby Hacks for New Dads

The Comprehensive Guide to Effortless Parenting,
Infant Care, and Baby Development

David Hall

© Copyright 2023 - All rights reserved.

The content contained within this book may not be reproduced, duplicated or transmitted without direct written permission from the author or the publisher.

Under no circumstances will any blame or legal responsibility be held against the publisher, or author, for any damages, reparation, or monetary loss due to the information contained within this book, either directly or indirectly.

Legal Notice:

This book is copyright protected. It is only for personal use. You cannot amend, distribute, sell, use, quote or paraphrase any part, or the content within this book, without the consent of the author or publisher.

Disclaimer Notice:

Please note the information contained within this document is for educational and entertainment purposes only. All effort has been executed to present accurate, up to date, reliable, complete information. No warranties of any kind are declared or implied. Readers acknowledge that the author is not engaged in the rendering of legal, financial, medical or professional advice. The content within this book has been derived from various sources. Please consult a licensed professional before attempting any techniques outlined in this book.

By reading this document, the reader agrees that under no circumstances is the author responsible for any losses, direct or indirect, that are incurred as a result of the use of the information contained within this document, including, but not limited to, errors, omissions, or inaccuracies.

Contents

Introduction

A lot of people dream of the day that they finally get to bring human life into this world. With the advancements in modern medicine, those who struggle with infertility are also able to enjoy every step of having a baby. Getting the baby here accounts for a fraction of the journey; the real leg work comes with raising the baby well. Some parents look like they have their ducks in a row, and the whole process of parenting comes easy to them. While that is good for them, this is not the case for everyone.

Some people will require some help in order to develop their parental instincts. If you consider what the role of parenting truly entails, it is understandable why most people will need some assistance. It doesn't matter if you are new at parenting or if you already have a few bundles of joy at home, everyone could benefit from some help.

Becoming a parent humbles you because you never know what's coming next. Parenting methods have evolved over the years. There are some good lessons in how prior generations brought up their young. It is important to discontinue using methods that have been proven to be detrimental to the growth of a child. Parenting hacks vary by generation and culture, so use what works for you and feel free to discard the rest.

There are different parenting hacks that are passed down from generation to generation that are actually quite harmful to children and babies. The classic example is putting a blanket over the open part of your baby stroller so that they are protected from the harmful rays of the sun. This hack is actually dangerous, and it can lead to your baby overheating. Contrary to popular belief, an ice bath will not break your child's fever, and it can cause your child to develop a life-threatening condition called "hypothermia."

Using whiskey on the gums to ease teething pain or using Benadryl as a sleep aid in order to sedate your small baby or child is incredibly harmful for your child, yet it is something that may be suggested to you by your grandparents. Be wary of the shortcuts they took that we know now to be hazardous and harmful to babies and young children. Ask your midwife, general practitioner, or your child's pediatrician if some of the old-school parenting methods sound suspicious to you. Some are actually harmless. Children are very resilient, but their lives are also quite fragile (Horn, 2018). It is better to be safe than to be sorry.

With the best interest of the child at heart, this book seeks to introduce you to "baby hacks" which is a unique and effective way of parenting that will not only fulfill the needs of your baby, but also take the load off of you. You may be familiar with the word "hack," as it has become quite popular in modern times.

Everyone is always looking for the next hack to make their life easier; this means that baby hacks will make your parenting journey exponentially easier. According to the Merriam-Webster Dictionary (2023), "hack" is best described as an innovative method that improves the way you do something, or a shortcut of sorts. There are so many websites and books dedicated to teaching various hacks to improve your daily tasks and quality of life. By aligning these various improved methods of doing things, you can save time, money, and effort in the way you perform daily tasks. Similarly, baby hacks can save you the headache of trying to figure out the best ways to care for your baby in certain scenarios, or how to approach certain problems using innovative solutions.

So, What Is a Baby Hack?

Most parents scramble for the advice of their parents or try to refer to information from various online forums and classes. The more information you have, the better. Parents today are fortunate because they live in a time where a mountain of information is available whenever you need it. Whether you decide to buy baby magazines, head to the local library to read up on parenthood, or purchase books online, you have the option of reaching out to various experts and people with experience to help you be a better parent. Information is available to you 24/7, if you have access to the internet. Type a question into Google, and you'll get insight into a plethora of topics in an instant.

The main goal of being a mother or father is to successfully raise your offspring to be contributing members of society. This means that you have to keep them safe and healthy until they are self-reliant. It's a monumental task that is immensely rewarding. It can also be intensely stressful at times.

You are tasked with changing every stinky diaper, preparing every bottle and meal for your little one, administering medicine, and protecting them from harm until they are able to do so for themselves. The tasks you have to perform as a parent are not always easy or intuitive, but rather beg the question of *how* you will do them.

"Baby hacks" refer to clever tricks and tips that can be used in child rearing. For example, parents who are struggling with a baby who has colic are advised to purchase colic drops to ease their infant's symptoms. A simple hack for colic is to rub your baby's belly clockwise and cycle their legs gently to release any trapped gas that could contribute to their discomfort, which may ease colic symptoms. Another hack to try for colic is to keep your baby swaddled with their arms and legs tucked into their swaddling blanket. You can find tutorial videos online that teach you how to swaddle your child safely so they do not overheat. If you've tried everything and nothing seems to work for your colicky baby, we hope you find relief soon. Colic typically disappears around the time your child turns four months old (*Colic*, 2023).

The good news is that there are hacks for every stage of parenting and by utilizing them you can achieve your parenting goals. Not only will you have a child that is developing well, but you will also reduce the stress and anxiety that naturally comes with parenting. There is so much pressure to be perfect when every parent should know that perfection is unachievable. It is impossible to be the perfect parent or raise your child to be the perfect kid because you are human and will make mistakes. Baby hacks are an easy way to ensure that both the parent and the child are happy and healthy.

Benefits of Baby Hacks

Parents today are juggling so many different hats. They have to work, navigate challenging economic conditions, and try to save money while caring for their parents. Adding the role of becoming a parent to the mix can be quite challenging. A lot of our parents tried to strike a balance between their career and home life, but this was not easy for them to achieve. Now, the struggle is yours.

Although it may be challenging, it is not impossible. A career-oriented woman who is climbing the corporate ladder can also be a caring, attentive mother. Any man who is striving to provide for his family can also fulfill the demanding role of being a more hands-on father. Any parent can help their partner manage household chores and finances in equal measures.

Finding an easier way to strike a balance between work and home life is the key to managing it all. Using baby hacks will ensure that you are not spending hours trying to accomplish a task that you could easily finish within minutes. If you spend less time trying to figure out the mundane stuff, you will have more time to pull yourself into your career goals, which will benefit the entire family. Baby hacks will allow you to have more time to spend with your baby, partner, or for other activities that give you fulfillment.

Parenting can make you feel terrible about yourself when things are just not going right. You can end up questioning your abilities by wondering if you are capable of this gargantuan task of raising this small human being. Parents of healthy newborns can often feel like they don't know what they're doing, especially if the baby cries for long periods of time even after being changed, fed, bathed, and dressed.

Or, consider the parents of a toddler who seems to have one tantrum after another. Experiencing these high-stress moments can leave you feeling mentally exhausted and with little faith in your parenting skills. Baby hacks can give you a boost in confidence where failed parenting techniques have eroded it. Once you witness these baby hacks at work, you will begin to regain faith in yourself as a parent and trust that you are competent enough to walk the parenting journey with your head held high.

There are so many joyful days that you will get to experience as a parent due to the many milestones your child will go through as they age. Watching them take their first steps, say their first word, and walk up to their first day of elementary school, college, and their wedding day is unbelievably rewarding as a parent. You played a significant part in the successes your child accomplishes.

You have a full life ahead filled with heart-warming memories. You will also have less than desirable, bone-deeply exhausting days because that is the unpredictable nature of parenting and life. Your child will get sick, and you will have to do everything within your power to make sure they are nursed back to good health. As your child gets older, their tantrums decrease, and certain other behaviors develop that become a thorn in your side. There is no avoiding it.

You have to jump in headfirst and try to muscle through the annoying, uncomfortable, and inconvenient days. No matter what you come across in your parenting journey, you have to keep going. Resilience is an essential parenting skill, and you have to learn it quite quickly. You have to keep trying different methods for various situations until you find the combination that works for your kid. You don't have the luxury to pause your parenting role. Baby hacks can help you become resilient so that you can give your children the best of yourself all the time.

Parenting requires you to be flexible. You can prepare for your baby down to the last detail, but that will not guarantee that things will go to plan. New mothers often go into painstaking detail when drawing out their birth plan; they have every right to be in control of what happens during the birth of their child and what happens to their body. Unfortunately, new parents quickly learn that they may have to improvise, as things do not always turn out the way any parent wants them to. Life is unpredictable.

Baby hacks teach you to be flexible and less rigid in the things that you desire. There are 1,000 ways to approach any given task, and you should be open to them all. This will also demonstrate how creative you can be to successfully raise children. It's okay to deviate from the traditions of your parents and grandparents to carve your own unique parenting style. You are under no obligation to follow the ways that are recommended by previous generations, or even those outlined in this book. These are all sources for you to pull from that will help make your parenting journey at least a bit easier.

The world is constantly evolving, and the parents of 20 to 30 years ago did not have to deal with what parents are dealing with today. Technology is changing the world at a rapid pace, and parents in previous years were not facing the challenges you now face. You are experiencing variables that have never been seen before.

Consider the role parents played during the initial stages of the COVID-19 pandemic when schools closed and caretakers everywhere had to step into the shoes of a teacher: It was unprecedented. Until the Zoom lessons took over, parents had to be their child's teacher and inch each child closer to their educational goals while working from home and trying to keep the family from going stir-crazy because the entire world was on lockdown. You need to be creative and deviate from the norm when the situation calls for it. Roll with the punches.

Introduction

Baby hacks provide great significance for numerous reasons, including safety. You have to make sure your baby or toddler is safe throughout the day. They pick up so many things, and their first instinct is to put it in their mouths. For example, the pool noodle hack can stop your baby from rolling out of the bed and sustaining injuries to their head or body while you quickly use the bathroom, make a meal, or take a shower when you are alone with your child. As much as you want to be at your baby's side 24/7, that is physically impossible. There are certain baby hacks that you can implement to keep your baby safe without taking on the neurotic role of having your baby under your constant supervision.

There is a gadget for everything. The list of things you need when preparing for a newborn baby is quite long and elaborate. It can be quite overwhelming. You may end up questioning if you are truly ready to be a parent. Some of the baby hacks that will be mentioned are low-cost or even free, which can be helpful if your family is on a budget. Everyone enjoys saving costs whenever they can because the cost of living has risen to such high levels. *Baby Hacks* will demonstrate how to parent without judgment. Always remember that what works, works. There is no perfect way to parent; therefore, try to leave any judgment at the door. The overall goal is to simplify the entire process of parenting so you can have more fun in your role as mum or dad.

Who Is This Book For?

If you are currently pregnant and expecting a bundle of joy, *Baby Hacks* is an invaluable resource to get your parenting journey started. You'll know what to expect throughout every step of the way so you can adequately prepare. If you've ever wondered how you are going to get through this exciting, but nerve-wracking, time, do not fear, as you have a competent guide in this book.

If this isn't your first rodeo, this book is also for you. You may benefit from the content in this book if you already have experience at parenting but are looking for more effective and creative ways to execute your role and responsibility in raising your child. As a parent, it is quite understandable that you are always looking for better balance in your life. You are dedicated to the lives of your children, but you also need to live your own life without getting consumed by the stress inherent in parenting. If you truly want to explore innovative parenting methods so that you can enjoy more time with your children and have better experiences in your own journey, read on and get ready to become rich because there is gold ahead.

Chapter 1

Preparing for Parenthood

Congratulations! You're going to have a baby! While this knowledge is exciting, it also fills you with anticipation for all the different things you need to get ready before the baby arrives. Not only should you prepare your environment for the coming of the newborn, but you have to prepare yourself as well. Perhaps your belly is swollen with the hope of a new life, or you're watching the days go by as your partner is carrying your new baby. Maybe your baby is arriving in other ways: Via adoption, fertility treatments, surrogacy, or through foster care. Any way that you become entrusted with raising and caring for a separate, small human being, you should be proud of your new role.

As a competent adult, you are cognizant of the fact that the onus is on you to make sure the arrival of this new addition to your family happens without a glitch. Preparing for the birth or arrival of a child can bring with it a rollercoaster of emotions. You may even be surprised at some of the feelings you might experience.

The first thing you experience is, obviously, excitement. When it begins to look like a sure thing that you are definitely having a baby, you may initially feel elated and exhilarated. The various images of you experiencing various milestones with your baby may flash in your mind. In these moments, you can't wait to meet your little one and start your journey as a parent. Soon after the excitement settles, nervousness may quickly follow. As the due date inches closer, your nerves may start to kick in as you wonder if you truly are prepared to take on this challenging, yet fulfilling, role of being a parent. You will be prone to worrying if everything goes smoothly and if you will be able to handle the sleepless nights and endless diaper changes. You will become apprehensive about every single aspect of parenting, wondering how your parents got through the feelings of edginess.

Anxious anticipation may have entered your mind as you continue to prepare for the coming of your small baby. Watching the pregnancy unfold and patiently waiting for the baby to arrive can feel similar to going to bed on Christmas Eve as a child. Curiosity can take hold as you wonder what your baby looks like and what it will feel like to hold them in your arms for the first time. Nine months can feel like a life-time. It is natural to feel impatient as the due date approaches. You may feel like you are ready for the baby to be born and can't wait any longer! While most of the feelings can be posi-tive feelings, you might also experience some trepidation. As much as you're looking forward to the birth of your child, you might experience anxiety about the process. Will labor be long and painful? Will the baby be healthy? Will everything go as planned? All the unknowns and variables can create a state of anxiousness that can really get you overthinking.

Luckily, because of medical advancements, you can maintain a sunny disposition because the midwives, nurses, and doctors know what they are doing. You can rest easy and put your faith in them that everything regarding the birth of your child will go well. Despite any fears or worries, there's always a sense of hope that everything will turn out the way that it's supposed to. You're hoping for a smooth delivery and a healthy baby. Finally, when the baby is born into the world, there's nothing but pure joy and elation. Every parent can attest to the magnitude of those first few minutes when you look at your baby and realize that they are finally here. Holding your baby for the first time is an indescribable feeling, and all of the emotions that led up to this moment are forgotten in an instant. You will only experience love and joy.

Preparing for the birth of a child can be a wild ride, but ultimately, it's one of the most humbling and rewarding experiences life has to offer. Aside from the emotions, you need to understand what is going on with your baby so that you can attempt to meet their needs. This chapter will focus on knowing exactly what the physical, emotional, and development needs of your baby are. Parenting is much easier in an environment that is safe and comfortable. You will be guided on grasping the significance of the home environment in promoting healthy growth and development in your baby as well as baby hacks to make your home baby-friendly. Further, there will be a discussion around car and traveling safety so that you can protect your baby even when you're on-the-go. Finally, this chapter will conclude with various things you can do to build a support system that will help you navigate the good and bad times of your parenting journey.

Understanding the Needs of a Newborn

As a parent of a newborn, the experience can consume you entirely. From the moment you hold your precious little one in your arms, your life changes forever. It feels amazing to be the parent of a newborn despite the challenges that come with it. From the first moment you hold your newborn, you will experience a rush of emotions all at once. You feel an exhilarating sense of love, joy, and gratitude, mixed with healthy amounts of fear, self-doubt, and anxiety. You're filled with a sense of awe and wonder as you look at the tiny, fragile being in your arms. The weight of the responsibility that comes with being a parent can feel overwhelming. Mostly, a sense of purpose and fulfillment like you've never experienced before will overcome you and be the motivating force that makes you want to be a good parent.

The first few weeks after bringing a newborn home can be incredibly challenging. The baby is growing and a lot is happening to them developmentally. These changes affect how the baby behaves. You have to try to predict what is happening and meet the baby's needs. You're in an adjustment period and it can prove extremely difficult not only for your baby, but you as well. Because you're adjusting to a new routine, expect that sleep deprivation will be at an all-time high. Constant exhaustion and emotional upheaval will be feelings that you need to learn to cope with. Mom is still recovering from childbirth, and her hormones are all over the place; dad has to deal with his normal life and somehow help mum through her recovery while also raising the newborn baby too. It's quite expected to feel anxious, scared, and overwhelmed during this time.

To be successful during this phase, one must understand what the needs of a newborn are. A newborn baby communicates their needs in a way that you may not understand. Certain motions and sounds will be indicators of what they need, and it is your job to decipher what they are trying to communicate. For example, different cries can mean different things; a high-pitched cry that doesn't stop even when comforted could mean your baby is hungry, or a more breathy cry could mean that your baby is tired and wants a nap. The needs of a newborn include their physical, emotional and developmental needs. It is important that you are aware of all of them so that you don't focus on one area and neglect other areas. Newborn babies do not understand that they are a completely separate person from their mother. During the first two months of their life, a newborn has no control over the movements that their body makes and any movement they do make is purely reflexive or involuntary. As your baby is constantly learning and taking in stimuli, they are also trying to signal to you what they need when they are hungry or tired. You have to keep up with the pace of development so that you can keep them loved, satisfied and happy.

Physical Needs

Having to care for a newborn baby brings with it a host of responsibilities, including meeting the physical needs of the newborn. As a caregiver, it is essential to understand the physical needs of a newborn to ensure their proper growth and development. This is where the heavy lifting of parenting takes place. Feeding, sleeping, and diapering will be discussed in detail in the following chapter.

- **Bathing**

Giving your newborn a bath can be an exciting experience for both you and your baby. However, it can also be a little nerve-wracking, especially for first-time parents. Even if you have some experience, it is still a little daunting. Newborns do not require daily bathing, as their skin is delicate and can dry out easily. It is best to bathe them two to three times a week using warm water and mild soap. It is also essential to ensure that the baby is not exposed to cold air or water during and after the bath. Follow these simple steps to bathe your newborn safely:

1. Before you begin, gather all the necessary supplies, including a baby bathtub or sink, mild baby soap, a soft washcloth, a towel, and a clean diaper. It's essential to have everything within reach to prevent leaving your baby unattended.

2. Choose a time when your baby is calm and alert and when you have enough time to give them your full attention. It's best to bathe your baby when they're not hungry or tired to make the process more comfortable for both of you.

3. Fill the bathtub or sink with warm water that's not too hot or cold. The ideal temperature for the water should be around 100°F (38°C). Test the water temperature with your elbow or the inside of your wrist to ensure it's not too hot.

4. Undress your baby and wrap them in a towel, leaving only the areas you plan to wash exposed.

5. Use a soft washcloth and mild baby soap to clean your baby's face, body, and hair. Be gentle and avoid getting soap or water in their eyes or mouth. Use a cup or your hand to pour water over your baby's body to rinse them off.

6. Once you've washed your baby, use a clean washcloth to rinse them off with clean water. Wrap them in a clean towel and gently pat them dry, paying extra attention to the folds and creases in their skin.

7. Dress your baby in a clean diaper and clothes, making sure they are warm and comfortable.

Remember that regular soap can irritate your baby's delicate skin, so use mild, unscented baby soap. Always support your baby's head and neck throughout the bath to prevent their head from falling forward or backward. Never overfill the tub, and always keep your baby within arm's reach to prevent accidents. Never leave your baby unattended during a bath, even for a moment. Giving your newborn a bath can be a fun bonding experience, but it's essential to do it safely and correctly. With these bathing hacks and a little practice, you can become a pro at bathing your newborn.

- **Clothing**

Newborns require appropriate clothing to keep them warm and comfortable. It is essential to dress the baby in well-fitting and breathable clothes, such as onesies, sleepers, and swaddling blankets. Avoid tight-fitting clothes that could restrict the baby's movement. Dressing your newborn can be both exciting and intimidating, but once you get the hang of things, it will come naturally to you as your baby gets older. Every parent has the most fun with buying their baby clothes because they are just so adorable. Newborns have delicate skin that needs gentle care, and they require clothing that is comfortable and safe. When choosing clothes for your newborn, opt for soft, breathable, and comfortable fabrics like cotton, bamboo, or other natural fibers. Avoid fabrics that are too rough or synthetic, which can irritate your baby's skin. Look for clothes that have snaps or zippers for easy access when changing diapers.

Do not overthink dressing your newborn; it doesn't have to be complicated. In the first few weeks, opt for simple outfits like onesies, rompers, and footed sleepers. Ditch the clothes that have too many buttons, snaps, or complicated designs that can be overwhelming to put on and take off. Keep outfits simple. Newborns are unable to regulate their body temperature effectively, so it's crucial to watch for signs of overheating. Avoid dressing your baby in too many layers, especially during warm weather. Check your baby's neck and back to ensure they're not sweating or overheating. Dress your baby appropriately for the weather. In warm weather, dress your baby in lightweight, breathable clothes, and in cold weather, add layers to keep them warm. Use hats and mittens to keep your baby's head and hands warm.

Your baby's clothes should be easy to remove and put back on so that you don't have to undress your baby entirely during diaper changes. Newborns grow quickly, so it's crucial to buy a variety of sizes, especially in the first few months. Newborn sizes may fit your baby for only a few weeks, so it's helpful to have larger sizes on hand. Remember to be gentle when dressing your newborn, as their skin is delicate and sensitive. Support your baby's head and neck and avoid pulling clothes over their head roughly. Dressing your newborn can be an enjoyable and rewarding experience if you dress your newborn comfortably.

Meeting the physical needs of a newborn is crucial for their growth and development. Providing adequate nutrition, a safe sleeping environment, frequent diaper changes, appropriate clothing, and regular bathing are some of the essential physical needs of a newborn. As a caregiver, it is essential to understand these needs and ensure that they are met to ensure the baby's wellbeing.

Emotional Needs

Newborns have emotional needs that are just as important as their physical needs. While they may not be able to communicate their feelings or needs verbally, they have ways of expressing themselves that parents and caregivers need to be aware of. Newborns need to bond with their parents and care-givers, and this starts from the moment they are born. Bonding helps to build trust, comfort, and security. You can bond with your newborn by holding them, talking to them, and making eye contact. Skin-to-skin contact is also an excellent way to bond with your newborn.

Newborns need to feel safe and secure. They may cry when they are hungry, tired, or uncomfortable. As a parent or care-giver, it's essential to respond to their needs promptly. You can comfort and soothe your newborn by holding them, rocking them gently, or using a pacifier. Singing, talking, and playing soft music can also be comforting for your newborn. Newborns need love and affection just as much as adults do. Show your newborn love and affection by cuddling, hugging, and kissing them. Responding to your newborn's needs with warmth and affection can help them feel loved and secure. Newborns are curious about the world around them and need stimulation to help them learn and develop. Simple things like colorful toys, mobiles, and rattles can provide stimulation and help develop their senses. Talking, singing, and reading to your newborn can also help stimulate their brain development.

Newborns are not aware of their environment or the things that they are going through. They are not even aware that they are a separate person from their mother. They have no idea who is caring for them or providing them food. They will cry because they feel like taking a nap or because they need to feed again. They have no idea that mom and dad are bending over backwards to meet their every desire. If you put yourself in the mindset of a newborn, you would understand that they are not trying to get attention by crying for extended periods of time. They don't have the mental capacity to spite anyone, and they are not out to get you. They have feelings but are not yet able to think. In about two months, they will probably be able to smile. Newborns will be laughing out loud within three months. Their emotional development seems random and demanding, but you will get through this phase. Take each day as it comes because the days will differ.

Establishing a predictable routine can help your newborn feel secure and comfortable. It's essential to maintain consistency in your newborn's daily routine, including feeding, sleeping, and playtime. Positive reinforcement can help encourage positive behavior in your newborn. Praising and smiling at your newborn when they do something positive can help reinforce good behavior and make them feel loved and valued. By providing a safe and secure environment, responding to their needs promptly, and showing them love and affection, you can help your newborn thrive emotionally.

Developmental Needs

There are certain things that you can do with your baby to deepen your bond and aid their developmental needs. Your baby's senses, brain, and body are constantly evolving and growing. By doing the following activities, you are supporting their developmental needs (*Child development (1)- newborn to three months*, 2021):

- Speak to your baby; tell them how much you love them. Get them used to hearing their name and what your voice sounds like. Face them so that they can watch your different expressions as you speak.
- Sing to your baby. It doesn't matter what you sing so long as you use a melodic tone that has a soothing effect on the baby.
- Find some classical music or smooth jazz to play for your baby. It will stimulate their sense of hearing

without overwhelming them. Try not to play music at a high volume but keep it at low levels so you don't overstimulate your baby.

- Create a colorful baby mobile that has different shapes and hang it above your baby's head in their cot.
- Imitate your baby's different expressions to see if they will react in any way.
- Touch your baby on different parts of their body, alternating the various types of touch from rubbing to gentle strokes. Take notice of the types of touch that they enjoy.
- Hold and cuddle your baby often.

By understanding the various needs you need to fulfill when caring for your newborn, you can lessen your own frustration and create a better routine for your newborn. There will be very few things that are a surprise to you as you may be able to anticipate your baby's needs better.

Creating a Baby-Friendly Home Environment

Creating a safe and comfortable home environment for your baby is essential to ensure their overall wellbeing and development. This will not only help in keeping the baby secure and healthy, but also contribute to their emotional and cognitive development. Firstly, it's essential to create a safe sleep environment for your baby to prevent the risk of sudden infant death syndrome (SIDS). Place your baby on their back to sleep, use a firm and flat mattress, and ensure that the crib meets the safety standards. Use a firm, flat mattress: A firm and flat mattress is the safest option for a newborn's sleep surface. Co-sleeping is not recommended, as it increases the risk of suffocation, entrapment, and SIDS. Instead, place your baby in their own crib or bassinet in your room for, at least, the first six months of their life. Ensure that the sleeping area is free from hazards such as loose bedding, soft objects, or toys. Use a fitted sheet to cover the mattress and avoid using bumper pads, sleep positioners, or other similar products.

Dress your baby appropriately for the temperature to avoid overheating or getting too cold. A good rule of thumb is to dress them in one layer more than you would wear in the same conditions. Maintaining cleanliness is essential to prevent the spread of germs and infections. Clean the baby's toys, clothes, and bedding regularly, but make sure to use baby-safe cleaning products. Babies are sensitive to temperature, so it's important to keep the temperature of the home at a comfortable level. Dress your baby in appropriate clothing for the weather and use a room thermometer to monitor the temperature. Limit the number of visitors to your home, especially during the first few weeks after your baby's birth. Ensure that visitors are not sick and ask them to wash their hands before holding the baby.

Babies are curious and love to explore their surroundings. Encourage exploration by providing safe and stimulating toys, books, and games. Create designated play areas that are easily accessible and free from hazards. The home environment can also play a crucial role in fostering social and emotional development. Create a warm and nurturing environment by providing plenty of love, attention, and affection. Respond to your baby's needs promptly and consistently and establish a predictable routine. Excessive screen time can have negative effects on a child's development. Limit screen time and provide plenty of opportunities for hands-on learning and exploration.

Baby-Proofing

Baby-proofing your home is crucial to prevent accidents and injuries. For example, you may have to install safety gates, corner protectors, outlet covers, or cabinet locks. Ensuring that electrical outlets are covered is also important. Remember to keep small objects and choking hazards out of reach. Here are some tips to help you babyproof your home:

1. Identify potential hazards in your home, such as sharp corners, loose cables, and breakable objects.
2. Secure heavy furniture, such as bookcases and dressers, to the wall to prevent them from tipping over.
3. Install safety gates at the top and bottom of stairs and in doorways to keep your baby from accessing unsafe areas.
4. Cover electrical outlets with safety plugs or outlet covers to prevent your baby from sticking their fingers or objects inside.
5. Install childproof locks on cabinets and drawers to keep your baby from accessing potentially dangerous items such as cleaning products and sharp objects.
6. Use door stoppers to prevent doors from slamming and potentially injuring your baby's fingers.
7. Install window guards to prevent your baby from falling out of open windows.
8. Secure cords from blinds and curtains to prevent your baby from getting tangled or pulling them down.
9. Store dangerous items such as medications, chemicals, and sharp objects out of reach or in locked cabinets.

10. Supervise your baby at all times. Even with baby
    proofing measures in place, it's essential to keep a
    watchful eye on your baby to prevent accidents.

When you create a safe and comfortable home environment
for your baby, you are building a foundation for their wellbeing and development. By following these practical tips and
advice, you can ensure that your baby feels secure, comfortable, and protected in their home. The parenting burden will
also be eased.

Car Safety

After your baby is born, you will need to take them home
from the hospital. Within their first week, your baby would
have ridden with you in the car. Unfortunately, it is not safe to
ride in the car with your baby in your arms. What if you are
alone, where will you put your baby? Car safety is critical for
babies because car accidents are one of the leading causes of
injury and death among infants. Properly securing your baby
in a car seat can significantly reduce the risk of injury or death
in the event of a car crash.

Make sure that you select a car seat that is appropriate for your
baby's age, weight, and height. There are three types of car
seats: Infant car seats, convertible car seats, and booster seats.
Choose a seat that fits your baby's needs and meets safety standards. The car seat manufacturers will indicate on the pack-
aging on the car seat which age group the car seat is suitable
for. Read the labels carefully before purchasing. The car seat
will come with a manual. Make sure to read the car seat
manual as well as your vehicle's owner manual to ensure that
the seat is installed correctly. If you are completely clueless,

you can have a certified child passenger safety technician check your installation.

Durbin & Hoffman (2018) recommends keeping babies in rear-facing car seats until they reach the highest weight or height allowed by the car seat manufacturer. This typically means rear-facing until at least two years of age. "Current estimates of child restraint effectiveness indicate that child safety seats reduce the risk of injury by 71% to 82% and reduce the risk of death by 28% when compared with children of similar ages in seat belts" (Durbin & Hoffman, 2018). Don't forget to buckle your baby in correctly every time you use the car seat. Ensure that the harness straps are snug and in the right position, and the chest clip is at armpit level. Avoid dressing your baby in bulky clothing while in the car seat, as it can interfere with the harness's proper fit. Instead, dress them in thin layers and use a blanket over the harness.

Check regularly for car seat recalls and register your car seat with the manufacturer to receive notifications. Always keep your baby in the back seat, preferably in the middle seat, as it is the safest position. Never leave your baby unattended in the car, even for a minute.

Factors To Consider When Choosing a Car Seat

If this is your first baby, you are probably overwhelmed by the numerous options of car seats. Choosing the right car seat and installing it correctly is crucial to ensure your baby's safety while traveling in a car. Consider the following factors when choosing the right car seat:

- The type of car seat. There are three types, namely infant, convertible, and booster seats. Infant car seats are suitable for babies up to 30 pounds or one year of age. Convertible car seats can be used in both rear-facing and forward-facing modes, and they are suitable for babies and toddlers weighing up to 65 pounds. Booster seats are used for children who have outgrown their convertible car seats and are at least four years old.

- The safety standards. Look for car seats that meet safety standards set by the National Highway Traffic Safety Administration (NHTSA) and the American Academy of Pediatrics (AAP).
- The fit. Choose a car seat that fits your baby's weight and height, and make sure that the seat's harness fits well against your baby's body.
- Is it a rear-facing seat? The American Academy of Pediatrics (AAP) recommends keeping babies in rear-facing car seats until they reach the highest weight or height allowed by the car seat manufacturer (until at least two years of age).

There are common challenges and concerns numerous parents encounter when it comes to child safety during travel in a passenger vehicle.

1. Airbags: Never place a rear-facing car seat in the front seat of a vehicle with an active airbag. If your vehicle has only one row of seats, deactivate the airbag or use a different vehicle.
2. Car seat expiration: Car seats expire, so check the expiration date before purchasing or using a car seat.
3. LATCH system: Many car seats come with a LATCH (Lower Anchors and Tethers for Children) system that allows you to attach the car seat to the vehicle without using the seatbelt. However, there are weight and age limits for using

the LATCH system, so make sure to read the car seat manual.
4. Multiple cars: If you have more than one car, consider purchasing an additional car seat base or a second car seat.

Of course, you can't always protect your baby from every external danger, but you can do your best to take some precautions to ensure their safety in the event of an accident.

Out and About Safety

You don't live in a vacuum and neither does your baby. You will need to make provision for their safety as you take them to the grocery store or visit with your sister. You already know how to keep yourself safe but there are certain things you can do to make sure your baby is safe too. As discussed earlier, car safety is critical when traveling with a baby. Make sure you have the appropriate car seat for your baby's age and weight and install it correctly. Avoid placing a rear-facing car seat in the front seat of a car with an active airbag. Check your car seat regularly for recalls and register it with the manufacturer. Further, choose a stroller that is appropriate for your baby's age and weight and has a secure harness. Always buckle up your baby and avoid hanging bags or heavy items on the stroller handles, as it can cause it to tip over.

Extreme temperatures can be dangerous for babies. In hot weather, keep your baby cool and hydrated by dressing them in lightweight clothing, providing plenty of fluids, and avoiding the sun during peak hours. In cold weather, dress your baby in layers and avoid prolonged exposure to extreme cold. When traveling with a baby, pack plenty of snacks and drinks. Choose foods that are easy to digest and avoid foods that can cause choking hazards, such as popcorn and nuts. If you are using a bottle, make sure to wash and sterilize it before each use. Babies have a weaker immune system than adults, so it's crucial to practice good hygiene when traveling. Wash your hands frequently and carry hand sanitizer with you. Avoid touching your baby's face, mouth, or eyes, and keep your baby away from sick people. Make sure anyone who touches the baby has either washed or sanitized their hands.

Preparing for trips with a baby can be a daunting task, but with proper planning, you can ensure that you are ready for any situation that may arise. Start preparations by making a list of everything you'll need for your baby, including clothing, diapers, wipes, formula, snacks, toys, and any other essential items. Pack extra of everything to be prepared for any unexpected situations. It may seem excessive, but you can never be sure what's going to happen. Learn as much as you can about your destination, including weather conditions, medical facilities, and any potential safety hazards. This will help you prepare for any situation that may arise. Plan for frequent breaks during long trips to allow your baby to stretch and move around. This will help keep them comfortable and avoid any discomfort or irritability.

Be prepared to change your plans if your baby needs a break or if something unexpected happens. It's better to be flexible and adjust your plans than to push through and risk your baby's safety and comfort. When you have a baby with you, you can plan, but don't be rigid because your baby can change everything at a moment's notice. Keep all your baby's essentials in a diaper bag or backpack that is easy to access. This will help you stay organized and avoid any last-minute scrambling. When traveling, your baby may have difficulty sleeping in an unfamiliar environment. Consider bringing your baby's familiar blanket or toy to provide comfort. Always follow safe sleep guidelines, such as placing your baby on their back to sleep and avoid co-sleeping or sharing a bed with your baby.

When out and about with your baby, there are also several safety concerns to be aware of. Here are some common safety concerns and tips for handling them.

- Stranger danger: Keep your baby close to you and never leave them alone, even for a moment. As they grow, teach your child to never talk to strangers and to always ask for help from a trusted adult if they need it.
- Traffic safety: Look left and right and make sure the road is clear before crossing with your infant or stroller. Use crosswalks whenever possible.
- Water safety: Keep a close eye on your baby around any bodies of water, including pools, lakes, and oceans. Never leave your baby unattended near water and consider using a life jacket for added safety.
- Sun safety: Protect your baby from the sun by dressing them in lightweight clothing, applying sunscreen, and using a hat and sunglasses. Avoid the sun during peak hours when possible.

Having these considerations in mind will make sure you can enjoy your time out of the house while your baby feels safe and secure. Although babies are unpredictable, if you make them feel as comfortable as possible, they might not get over-whelmed by the new environment which will give you a chance to enjoy your outing and show them off to family and friends.

Building a Support System

Having a newborn baby will be a joyous, but challenging, time in your life. It can be physically, emotionally, and mentally demanding, and having a strong support system is crucial to get you through this period. A support system consisting of family, friends, and professional resources can provide you with the necessary assistance and support to cope with the demands of a new baby.

Family members are often the first line of support for new parents. They can help with the practical aspects of taking care of a newborn baby, such as cooking meals, cleaning, and doing laundry. Family members can also provide emotional support and advice, as they have likely gone through the same experience themselves. They can offer guidance on issues such as breastfeeding, sleeping patterns, and baby care. Having family members around can also help you when you need a break and some time for yourself. We all react differently to parenting; some people can go through it without getting emotionally exhausted, while other people get completely flustered. Don't ignore the alarm bells if you are at your limit.

Secondly, friends can be an invaluable source of support for new parents. They can provide emotional support, help with the practical aspects of baby care, and offer much-needed companionship. Friends can also offer a different perspective on the challenges of parenting, which can be helpful when new parents are feeling overwhelmed. Friends who are also parents can provide additional advice and guidance, based on their own experiences.

Thirdly, professional resources, such as midwives, lactation consultants, and pediatricians, can be essential in ensuring the health and wellbeing of both the baby and the mother.

Midwives can provide support and guidance throughout the pregnancy and postpartum period, including assistance with breastfeeding, nutrition, and mental health. Lactation consultants can provide support and guidance on breastfeeding, which can be challenging for some new mothers. Pediatricians can monitor the baby's growth and development, identify any health concerns, and provide guidance on baby care.

Finally, a strong support system can also help you manage the stress and anxiety that often comes with caring for a newborn baby. Parenting can be a lonely and isolating experience and having a support system can reduce feelings of loneliness and provide a sense of community. With an effective support system, you can also manage your mental health better, which is essential for both you and your baby.

Now, the hard work begins; who can serve as a resource in your support system? Building a supportive network as a new parent can be challenging, as it involves connecting with other parents, building relationships with professionals, and creating a community of support around you. This section offers practical activities that will guide you on what to do to build this support system.

1. Joining parenting groups or attending parenting classes can be a great way to meet other parents and build relationships with professionals. Look for local parenting groups or classes offered by hospitals, community centers, or parenting organizations. These groups provide a safe space to share experiences, ask questions, and connect with others who are going through similar experiences.
2. Attending baby and toddler groups can be an excellent way to connect with other parents and children in your community. Check out local groups

that meet regularly, such as parent and baby groups, playgroups, or music classes. These groups provide an opportunity to socialize, share experiences, and learn from other parents.

3. The internet can be a valuable resource for new parents. Look for online parenting forums or social media groups that focus on topics such as breastfeeding, sleep training, or baby care. These online communities provide a platform to ask questions, share experiences, and connect with others who are going through similar experiences.

4. Connecting with professionals, such as midwives, lactation consultants, or pediatricians, can provide you with guidance, support, and valuable resources. Take advantage of their expertise and ask questions or seek advice when needed.

5. Don't be afraid to ask family and friends for support. They can provide practical support, such as cooking meals or helping with housework, as well as emotional support when needed. Building a strong relationship with your partner can also provide much-needed support and a sense of shared responsibility.

6. If you are struggling with mental health issues, such as postpartum depression or anxiety, attending a support group can be a helpful way to connect with others and seek support. Look for local support groups for new parents or speak to your healthcare provider about resources in your area.

7. Taking care of yourself is essential for building a supportive network. Make time for self-care activities, such as exercise, meditation, or relaxation techniques. Prioritizing your own wellbeing can help you to be more present and engaged with your baby,

which can, in turn, help you build a stronger support network.

Building a supportive network as a new parent takes time, effort, and a willingness to seek out resources and connect with others. Don't rush the process. Remember that you are not the first person to go through this process. Listen to advice from others and be open to trying new things. By joining parenting groups, attending baby and toddler groups, seeking out online resources, connecting with professionals, utilizing family and friends, attending support groups, and taking care of yourself, you can create a community of support that can help you navigate the challenges of parenting a newborn.

Once you understand the needs of a newborn and how to care for them properly, half the battle is won. The more you perform the activities needed to care for your baby, the more confident you will become. You will also begin to learn what they prefer during bath time and bedtime or how they like to be spoken to. This is truly a time of discovery. Take every action as information when you are learning your child.

Chapter 2
Infant Care Basics

Caring for your infant properly is incredibly important for a multitude of reasons. Not only does it help ensure their physical health and development, but it also plays a vital role in their emotional wellbeing and the establishment of a strong bond between parent and child. First and foremost, proper infant care is essential for their physical health and development. Infants are extremely vulnerable and require a high level of care to ensure their basic needs are met. This includes things like feeding, diaper changing, and maintaining a safe sleep environment. Failure to provide these basic needs can result in serious health consequences, such as malnutrition, dehydration, and even death. Additionally, proper infant care is necessary to promote healthy physical development. This includes things like tummy time to help build neck and core muscles, as well as providing adequate stimulation to promote cognitive and sensory development.

In addition to physical health, proper infant care is also crucial for emotional wellbeing. Infants require a secure and nurturing environment to thrive emotionally. This means providing consistent care, love, and attention, as well as responding to their cries and other communication. Failure to provide this type of environment can lead to emotional distress, anxiety, and even long-term mental health problems. Furthermore, proper care plays an important role in the establishment of a strong bond between parent and child. Bonding is crucial for a child's emotional development, and it helps to promote a sense of security and trust that can last a lifetime. By providing consistent care and attention, parents can build a strong foundation for their relationship with their child. This can help to promote healthy communication and a strong sense of attachment between parent and child. The early years of a child's life are a critical period for brain development, and the experiences they have during this time can shape their future cognitive, emotional, and social development.

This chapter will be focused on what you can do to adequately care for the infant to create a solid foundation for their development. Simplifying these basic tasks will leave more time for you to care for yourself, do household chores, and spend quality time bonding with your baby.

Simplifying Feeding Routines

You are responsible for feeding your baby. Feeding is one of the most crucial physical needs of a newborn. During the first few months of life, a newborn requires frequent feedings of breast milk, formula, or sometimes, a combination of both. Breast milk is considered the best source of nutrition for a newborn, as it provides all the necessary nutrients and antibodies required for growth and development. Breastfeeding is also praised, as it strengthens the bond between a mother and her baby. If breastfeeding is not possible, formula milk can be given as an alternative. It is essential to feed the newborn on demand and not restrict them to a particular schedule.

Breastfeeding

Breastfeeding is the natural process of providing nourishment to a newborn baby through the mother's milk. It has numerous benefits for both the baby and mother. For thousands of years, this has been the preferred method of feeding a baby. Breastfeeding provides the baby with the ideal food for their growth and development. It contains all the necessary nutrients, such as protein, fat, carbohydrates, and vitamins that a newborn needs in the right proportions.

Breast milk also contains antibodies that help protect the baby from various infections, such as ear infections, respiratory infections, and meningitis. Breastfed babies also have a lower risk of developing chronic conditions, such as asthma, allergies, and obesity. There are significant benefits for the mother's health as well. It helps the uterus contract after birth, reducing the risk of postpartum bleeding. Breastfeeding also reduces the risk of breast and ovarian cancer, type 2 diabetes, and cardiovascular diseases. Additionally, breastfeeding mothers tend to return to their pre-pregnancy weight faster than those who do not breastfeed.

Nursing an infant also has significant benefits for society as a whole. It reduces the cost of healthcare for both the baby and mother by reducing the risk of illnesses and chronic conditions. The burden on the environment is reduced, as there is less waste produced if you aren't formula feeding. Breastfeeding also helps to establish a strong bond between the mother and baby. It promotes skin-to-skin contact, which helps regulate the baby's body temperature and heart rate. It also promotes emotional bonding, which is essential for the baby's overall development. However, despite the numerous benefits of breastfeeding, many women face challenges in breastfeeding, such as lack of support, discomfort, and cultural stigma. Therefore, it is essential to provide education and support to new mothers to help them overcome these challenges and make informed decisions about feeding their babies.

It is important to recognize that not all mothers are able to breastfeed, and there is nothing wrong with this. Some mothers may have medical conditions that prevent them from producing enough milk or make it difficult to breastfeed, while others may have personal reasons for not breastfeeding. In these cases, formula feeding is a perfectly acceptable alternative that can provide the necessary nutrition for the baby's growth and development. It is essential for mothers to make informed decisions about feeding their babies that are based on their individual circumstances and needs. Ultimately, what matters most is that the baby is fed and receives the necessary nutrition to thrive, whether through breast milk or formula.

Hunger Cues

Babies are not yet able to communicate their hunger verbally, so it is up to you to look for clues and signals that indicate that your baby needs to be fed. The rooting reflex is an instinctual response that newborns have when they are hungry (*Rooting reflex definition*, 2023). When a baby is hungry, they will turn their head towards anything that touches or strokes their cheek. This reflex helps the baby locate the mother's nipple for breastfeeding. If you notice your baby turning their head towards your chest or hand, it is probably a sign that they are hungry. Another sign to look out for to tell if your baby is hungry is when they start sucking on anything they can find, such as their fingers or a pacifier. The sucking reflex is a sign that your baby is ready to feed. If you don't pick up on these subtle cues, your baby will find a more extreme way of telling you that they need to eat.

Smacking or licking their lips could indicate that your baby is ready to feed again. This behavior is a result of the baby's anticipation of food. If you notice your newborn smacking their lips, it is a sign that they are ready for some milk. Increased activity like moving their arms and legs more vigorously, and wide-open eyes may be signs of hunger. When hunger has not been detected your baby may begin to cry. This is how your baby communicates that they need to be fed immediately. The loud screams and wailing indicate the urgency of the matter. However, it is not advisable to wait for the baby to cry, as this can lead to stress and anxiety for both the baby and you. Try your best to notice the earlier signs of hunger, such as rooting or sucking, before they get to the crying stage.

Proper Nutrition

The first year of your baby's life is a critical time for growth and development. Proper nutrition during this time is essential to ensure that your infant gets all the necessary nutrients for their growth and development. There are various guidelines for what is recommended for your baby at various stages of their infancy, and they include (*Breastfeeding*, 2023):

- Exclusively breastfeeding for six months. Breast milk is the best source of nutrition for a newborn baby. It provides all the necessary nutrients and antibodies required for growth and development. Breastfeeding should be done on demand, but if it is not possible, formula milk can be given as an alternative.

- Introducing solid foods. The introduction of solid foods should be done gradually, starting at around six months of age. The first foods to be introduced should be single-grain cereals, followed by pureed fruits and vegetables. It is recommended to introduce one new food at a time to watch for any allergic reactions or digestive issues. Try one new food, skip a week, then introduce a new one so you can track how your baby reacts to certain foods, if at all.

- Giving fruits and vegetables. These are an essential part of a baby's diet, as they provide vitamins, minerals, and fiber that are necessary for the rapid growth and development. Think about all the different parts of your baby's body that are constantly changing; your baby's body needs all the help it can get. Pureed or mashed fruits and vegetables can be introduced gradually, starting with a small amount and gradually increasing as your baby gets used to the taste and texture. One spoon every other day can get them used to the texture, taste, and smell of food.

- Pureed or mashed meats, poultry, fish, and tofu can be introduced at around eight months of age because protein is indispensable to your baby's growth and development. Eggs can be introduced after six months, starting with the yolk, followed by the white.

- Dairy products such as cheese, yogurt, and cottage cheese can be introduced at around eight months of age. It is recommended to introduce these foods gradually, starting with a small amount and gradually increasing as the baby gets used to the taste and texture. Be cautious of any gastrointestinal distress these foods may cause, as this may signal that your baby is lactose intolerant.

For more information, you can approach your local health care facility to receive advice from a midwife, pediatrician, or dietician on how to meet the needs of your baby.

Common Challenges

Feeding time can be a challenging experience for both baby and parent, particularly in the early months of a baby's life. As a new parent you may struggle to find the right feeding routine, while your baby may experience difficulties with latching, swallowing, and digestion. One of the most common challenges you may encounter is establishing a feeding routine that works for both the baby and your schedule. A feeding routine is important for both the baby's nutrition and establishing a predictable schedule for the caregiver. You should try to feed your baby on demand, which means feeding whenever the baby shows signs of hunger, such as rooting, sucking on their fists, or crying. It is also important to make sure the baby is getting enough milk at each feeding, which can be determined by monitoring the baby's weight gain and diaper output. You can also consider pumping breast milk or using formula to allow other caregivers to participate in feeding and establish a more flexible feeding routine.

Another common challenge is difficulty with latching, which can make breastfeeding painful and frustrating for both the baby and the mother. To overcome this challenge, mothers should try different positions and techniques, such as cradling, football hold, or side-lying positions, to find the most comfortable position for both the baby and mother.

They can also consult a lactation consultant or attend a breastfeeding support group to get guidance on improving their breastfeeding technique. For mothers who are unable to breastfeed, finding the right formula can also be a challenge. It is important to choose a formula that is appropriate for the baby's age, nutritional needs, and any special requirements, such as hypoallergenic or lactose-free formulas. Parents should also follow the instructions on the formula label carefully to ensure the right proportion of water and formula powder.

Babies may also experience difficulties with swallowing, reflux, and colic, which can cause discomfort and distress during feeding.

> Feeding is an important part of the everyday life of infants and young children, and much parent-child interaction occurs at feeding times. About 25% to 40% of infants and toddlers are reported by their caregivers to have feeding problems, mainly colic, vomiting, slow feeding, and refusal to eat (Bernard-Bonnin, 2006, para. 9).

To overcome these challenges, you can try different feeding positions, such as holding the baby upright or inclined, or taking breaks during feeding to allow the baby to burp or rest. You can also consult a pediatrician to get guidance on using medications or other remedies to alleviate the baby's symptoms. In addition to these challenges, feeding time can also be a source of stress and fatigue, particularly in the early months when the baby may need to be fed every few hours. To make feeding time easier, you can try the following tips:

- Create a calm and relaxing environment. Dim the lights, play soothing music, and minimize distractions to help the baby feel relaxed and focused on feeding.

- Use feeding as bonding time. Make eye contact, talk to the baby, and cuddle them during feeding to promote bonding and create a positive association with feeding.
- Prepare in advance. Have all the necessary supplies, such as bottles, formula, burp cloths, and a comfortable chair or cushion, ready before feeding time.
- Take breaks. It is important to take breaks during feeding to rest and recharge, particularly for mothers who are breastfeeding. Other family members or caregivers can help take over feeding duties to allow parents to rest.
- Seek support. It is important to seek support from family, friends, or support groups to help overcome feeding challenges and provide emotional support during this challenging time.

Every baby is different, so what you feed your baby will only be discovered as you care for your infant. Be kind during the breastfeeding stage, whether the mother is able to or not. You have your baby's pediatrician or your midwife to ask for advice in case you need professional assistance.

Making Diaper Changes Easier

Your newborn requires frequent diaper changes as they pass urine and stool frequently. They are not yet able to control their bladder and rectal sphincter. It is essential to know how and when to change your baby's diaper to avoid diaper rash and skin irritation. The use of gentle wipes and diaper rash cream can also help prevent skin irritation. Changing diapers is a critical skill that all new parents must master; you can't dodge it. Proper diaper changing ensures that your baby is clean, comfortable, and healthy. Before you begin, gather all the necessary supplies, including a fresh diaper, wipes, diaper cream, and a changing pad or towel. This will help keep everything organized and within reach. Choose a safe and comfortable place to change your baby, such as a changing table or a bed. Always use a changing pad or towel to protect your baby and the surface you are using. Since your baby has no control of their bowels, anything can happen. Be prepared.

Place your baby on their back with their legs up and gently hold their ankles with one hand. Use the other hand to remove the dirty diaper. This maneuvering will take some practice and may get harder as your baby gets stronger. Use wipes or a wet washcloth to clean your baby's bottom, wiping from front to back to prevent infections. If your baby has a diaper rash, apply a thin layer of diaper cream to the affected area. Slide the clean diaper under your baby, making sure the back of the diaper is aligned with their waist. Pull the front of the diaper up between your baby's legs and fasten the tabs on the sides. Roll up the dirty diaper, secure it with the tabs, and then dispose of it in a diaper pail or trash can. Always wash your hands thoroughly after changing a diaper to prevent the spread of germs. Some diapering hacks to consider include:

- Always making sure the diaper is snug, but not too tight. You should be able to fit one or two fingers between the diaper and your baby's skin.
- Change your baby's diaper as soon as it becomes soiled or wet to prevent diaper rash and infections.
- Keep an eye on your baby's skin for signs of diaper rash, such as redness, irritation, or bumps. If you notice these signs, apply diaper cream and change the

diaper more frequently. You can choose to allow your baby to go without a diaper for an hour or two to reduce irritation.

- If your baby is a boy, place a clean diaper over his genitals while changing him to prevent him from accidentally urinating on himself and/or on you.

With some practice, you will be able to change a diaper efficiently without struggling or taking too long.

Choosing the Right Diaper Brand

Choosing the right diaper brand for your baby can be overwhelming, especially for new parents who may not be familiar with the different types and brands available in the market. The following are some factors to consider when selecting a diaper brand for your baby.

- The size of the diaper is an important factor to consider to ensure a snug and comfortable fit for your baby. Look for diapers that are designed for your baby's weight and age to prevent leaks and discomfort.
- Diapers that have high absorbency are important to keep your baby dry and prevent rashes. Look for diapers that have multiple layers and are designed to absorb both urine and feces.
- Diapers are made from different materials, including cloth, disposable, and biodegradable materials. Each material has its benefits and drawbacks, so choose a material that suits your lifestyle, budget, and environmental concerns.
- Some babies may be sensitive to certain materials or chemicals used in diapers, which can cause skin

irritations or rashes. Choose a brand that is hypoallergenic and free of fragrances, dyes, and other chemicals that may irritate your baby's skin.

- Look for diaper brands that have a good reputation for quality and safety. Read reviews from other parents, talk to your pediatrician, and research the brand's safety record and certifications.
- Diapers can be expensive, so it's important to choose a brand that fits your budget. Consider buying in bulk or subscribing to a diaper delivery service to save money.
- Choose a diaper brand that is convenient for you to use, whether it's easy to find in stores, has a user-friendly design, or comes with useful features like wetness indicators or stretchy waistbands.

Choosing the right diaper brand for your baby requires careful consideration. By taking the time to research and compare different brands, you can find a diaper that meets your baby's needs and your family's budget and lifestyle. Remember to always prioritize your baby's comfort and safety when choosing a diaper brand.

Types of Stool

Stool consistency and color can be a useful indicator of a baby's health and digestion. It is important for you to monitor a baby's stool to ensure that they are getting the necessary nutrients and that their digestive system is functioning properly. The first stool that a baby passes after birth is called "meconium." Meconium is a dark, sticky, and tar-like substance that is usually passed within the first 24 hours of birth. It is made up of amniotic fluid, mucus, and intestinal cells that the baby ingested while in the womb. Meconium is usually odorless and does not contain any bacteria or digestive enzymes. As the baby starts to feed, their stool will change in consistency and color. Breastfed babies typically have stools that are soft, yellow, and seedy in texture. The color may vary from bright yellow to a mustard-like color, and the texture may be runny or curdled. This is because breast milk is easily digested and contains natural laxatives that help move the stool through the baby's digestive system.

Formula-fed babies, on the other hand, typically have stools that are thicker and have a paste-like consistency. The color may range from light brown to dark brown, and the smell may be stronger than breastfed baby stools. Formula-fed babies may also have fewer bowel movements than breast-fed babies. Green stools may indicate that the baby is getting too much foremilk, which is the thinner milk that comes first during breastfeeding. Foremilk is high in lactose and can cause the baby to have loose, green stools. If the baby is not getting enough hindmilk, which is the thicker, more nutrient-rich milk that comes later during breastfeeding, they may also have green stools.

Red stools may indicate that there is blood in the stool, which can be a sign of a more serious condition. Blood in the stool may be caused by a milk protein allergy or intolerance, a bacterial infection, or a tear in the baby's anus. If a baby has red stools, parents should seek medical attention immediately. White or clay-colored stools may indicate a blockage in the baby's bile duct or liver problems. Bile is a fluid produced by the liver that helps digest fats, and a blockage in the bile duct can prevent the bile from reaching the intestines and cause the stool to become white or clay colored. If a baby has white or clay-colored stools, parents should seek medical attention immediately.

Black or tarry stools may indicate that there is blood in the baby's digestive system, which can be a sign of a more serious condition. Black or tarry stools may also be caused by iron supplements or medications. If a baby has black or tarry stools, parents should seek medical attention immediately. Mucus in the stool may be caused by a viral or bacterial infection, or an allergy to certain foods. If a baby has mucus in their stool, parents should monitor their other symptoms, such as fever or vomiting, and seek medical attention if necessary. Foamy or frothy stools may indicate that the baby is getting too much lactose, which can cause the stool to become foamy or frothy. Foamy or frothy stools may also be caused by a bacterial infection or other digestive problems. You need to keep a keen eye on the contents of your baby's diaper so you can assess if your baby is having healthy bowel movements.

Common Challenges

Diapers are an essential part of caring for an infant, but they can also come with a few challenges. The following are some common challenges that parents may encounter when using diapers for their infants, starting with diaper rash. This is a common problem that occurs when the skin is exposed to moisture and friction from the diaper. It can cause redness, itching, and discomfort for the baby. To prevent diaper rash, change your baby's diaper frequently, use a barrier cream, and avoid using harsh wipes or soaps. Another challenge to overcome is leaks, which can occur when the diaper is not the right size or is not put on correctly. They can also happen when the diaper is not absorbent enough or is too full. To prevent leaks, choose the right size and brand of diaper, ensure a snug fit around the legs and waist, and change the diaper frequently.

Blowouts occur when the contents of the diaper leak out of the diaper and onto the baby's clothes or skin. They can happen when the diaper is too small or too loose, or when the baby has a bowel movement that exceeds the diaper's capacity. To prevent blowouts, choose the right size and brand of diaper, ensure a snug fit, and change the diaper promptly after a bowel movement. Some babies may be allergic to the materials or chemicals used in diapers, which can cause skin irritation or rashes. To prevent allergic reactions, choose a hypoallergenic brand of diaper, avoid using scented wipes or lotions, and change the diaper frequently. Diapers can emit an unpleasant odor, especially when they are soiled or left in the trash for too long. To prevent diaper smells, dispose of soiled diapers promptly, use a diaper pail with a tight-fitting lid, and consider using odor-reducing products like baking soda or charcoal filters.

Using diapers can present a few challenges when caring for an infant, but with the right techniques and products, these challenges can be easily managed. Be open to changing brands if the one you are currently using is not working for your baby or your pocket. If you encounter persistent or severe problems with your baby's diapers, consult your pediatrician for advice and treatment.

Creating a Comfortable Sleep Environment

Although newborns require a lot of sleep to aid their physical development, they often have trouble sleeping for long periods of time. These short sleep cycles can often leave both you and your baby feeling tired and frustrated. Newborns sleep for extended periods, typically for 16-17 hours a day. However, they do not have a fixed sleeping pattern and may wake up frequently to feed. It is essential to provide a safe and comfortable sleeping environment for the baby. The baby's sleeping area should be free from any objects that could suffocate the baby, such as pillows, blankets, or toys. It is also recommended to place the baby on their back to sleep to prevent sudden infant death syndrome (SIDS). You may be wondering if there is anything you can do to improve your baby's sleeping patterns. Fortunately, there are several things you can do to help your newborn sleep better.

Firstly, establish a bedtime routine. This allows the baby to anticipate what is going to happen and what sleep cues are. You are essentially helping your baby's body recognize when it is time to sleep. The trick is to do the same things in the same order at the same time every single night. A simple routine such as a warm bath, massage, and a lullaby can help the baby relax and prepare for sleep. Secondly, swaddle your baby. When the baby was still in the womb, the limited space felt comforting, like a hug. Swaddling is a technique that involves wrapping the baby tightly in a blanket. Swaddling can help the baby feel secure and prevent them from being disturbed by their own startle reflex. They are also familiar with this feeling, as they spent the last few months 'swaddled' in the womb.

Thirdly, try to ensure the room that the baby sleeps in is dark, cool and quiet during their sleep times. If you are unable to create a completely quiet environment, you could try to use white noise to drown out any noise. "White noise" is defined in the Merriam-Webster Dictionary as "a constant background noise, especially one that drowns out other sounds" (*White noise*, 2023). Searching white noise on YouTube or using a white noise app can help to keep your baby sleeping for longer. Lastly, cuddle and soothe the baby when necessary. Skin-to-skin contact can help the baby settle and feel loved. Talk to the baby in a calming, low voice to reassure them. Newborns often sleep better when they feel comforted and held. Rocking the baby gently or holding them close can help soothe them and promote better sleep.

Adjusting your life around your newborns sleeping patterns might drive you crazy in the beginning, especially if it is your first baby. When you have had experience with a newborn, you have an idea of what to expect, even though this doesn't lessen the torture of functioning on little to no sleep. When you don't get enough sleep, it can affect various areas of your life. Sleep deprivation can affect mood, concentration, and overall health. To reduce the negative effects of sleep deprivation, you can sleep when the baby sleeps. You may be tempted to get some chores in and clean up around the house, but the priority is your mental and physical wellbeing. This is a common piece of advice, but it is essential. Sleeping when the baby sleeps can help you get some much-needed rest and help you feel more refreshed when you wake up. Learn to nap when the baby sleeps.

Practicing good sleep hygiene can help improve the quality of your sleep. Quality is always more important than quantity. A few hours of good quality sleep are more valuable than four or five hours of broken, low-quality sleep. Good sleep hygiene includes creating a comfortable sleep environment, avoiding caffeine and alcohol before bed, and limiting screen time before bed. Incorporating a self-care routine can also improve sleep. Make time for activities that you enjoy, such as reading a book, painting or taking a relaxing bath. Self-care can help reduce stress and promote relaxation. Learn early on to accept help from your friends and family. During these difficult times, they can help relieve some of the burden of caring for a newborn. Your loved ones can help with tasks, such as cooking, cleaning, or caring for the baby, while you take some time to get some rest.

Keep communication lines open between you and your partner. Talk about how you are feeling and what you need. Creating a cohesive team of caregivers can help to keep stress levels and a minimum and promote better sleep for both of you. If you are struggling with sleep deprivation or think it has escalated to insomnia, it is essential to seek professional help. Talk to your healthcare provider about your concerns, and they may be able to offer guidance and support. It may feel like absolute torture when you are going through it, but remember, sleep deprivation is temporary, and things will get better with time.

The basics of caring for an infant include feeding them well, making sure their diapers remain dry and empty as well as ensuring they get enough sleep. Getting into the rhythm of things will get easier every day. Be patient with your baby and with yourself. Once you figure out what to feed your baby and which diapers work well, they will sleep for longer, and so will you.

Chapter 3
Baby Development

It only takes a year for your baby to undergo a remarkable transformation from a helpless newborn to an active toddler. As babies develop and change rapidly, each month brings novel and thrilling advancements. New parents may feel uncertain about what to expect next and how to determine if their baby's development is on track. However, it's crucial to recognize that each baby progresses at their own pace, and there is a significant "window" for reaching specific developmental milestones. Dr. Jennifer Shu, a pediatrician and co-author of "Heading Home with Your Newborn," notes that if a baby reaches one milestone earlier, they may achieve another milestone later since they're concentrating on perfecting the first skill (Shaw, 2009). For instance, some babies may utter their first word at eight months, whereas others may not speak until after their first birthday. Likewise, walking can begin anywhere from nine to 18 months.

Therefore, it's essential to keep these variations in mind while tracking your baby's development. It is an exhilarating experience to witness your infant grow and develop through various stages during their first year of life. From their first smile to the moment they start crawling, every milestone feels like a victory worth celebrating. As you watch your little one progress, you become amazed at their newfound abilities and curious about what they will do next. The excitement builds as you eagerly anticipate their first words, their first steps, and all the other magical moments that come with each stage of development. It's a thrilling journey that you get to share with your child, and the joy and wonder of it all make every sleepless night and every challenging moment completely worthwhile.

Physical Development

Physical development is an essential aspect of a child's growth and overall wellbeing. As babies grow, they undergo several stages of development that require proper care, nourishment, and support. There are different stages of physical development in babies, and there are different hacks you can use for promoting healthy growth and development. The first stage of physical development in babies is the newborn stage, which lasts from birth to around one month. During this stage, babies sleep for most of the day, but they gradually become more active and responsive to their environment. At this stage, it is crucial to ensure that the baby is getting enough nutrition, warmth, and rest. You can promote healthy growth by providing a safe and comfortable environment and feeding your baby breast milk or formula.

The second stage is the infant stage, which lasts from one month to 12 months. At this stage, babies start to develop their motor skills, including rolling, crawling, sitting, and standing. They also develop their senses, such as vision, hearing, and taste. It is essential to provide babies with plenty of opportunities to explore their environment, such as tummy time, which helps them develop their neck, back, and shoulder muscles. You can also promote healthy growth by providing age-appropriate toys, introducing solid foods at six months, and establishing a consistent sleep routine.

The third stage is the toddler stage, which lasts from one to three years. At this stage, toddlers continue to develop their motor skills, language, and cognitive abilities. They become more independent and curious, and it is essential to provide them with a safe environment that allows them to explore and play. You can promote healthy growth by encouraging physical activity, providing healthy meals and snacks, setting boundaries and routines, and providing age-appropriate toys and books. It is essential to provide a safe and nurturing environment, encourage physical activity and exploration, and establish routines that support healthy sleep, nutrition, and development. With proper care and support, babies can grow into healthy, happy, and thriving toddlers.

Encouraging movement and physical activity is crucial for promoting healthy growth and development in babies. Here are some hacks on how to encourage movement and activity while also considering safety during playtime:

1. Tummy time is an essential activity for babies as it helps them develop their neck, back, and shoulder muscles. You can encourage tummy time by placing your baby on a blanket or mat on the floor and getting down on the floor with them. You can also use toys or mirrors to keep your baby engaged during tummy time.
2. Babywearing is a great way to keep babies close while still allowing them to move and explore. Baby carriers or slings can provide a safe and comfortable way to

carry babies while also allowing them to move their arms and legs freely.

3. Play gyms are an excellent way to encourage movement and activity in babies. Play gyms typically have a soft, cushioned base with toys and activities hanging overhead that babies can reach for and interact with.

4. Crawl tunnels can be a fun way to encourage babies to move and explore. Crawl tunnels can be made from soft materials, such as blankets, or can be purchased from baby stores.

When it comes to playtime, safety is also essential. Babies should always be supervised during playtime. You should be within arm's reach of your baby at all times to ensure their safety. Toys should be age-appropriate and free from any choking hazards. You should always inspect toys for any small parts or pieces that could be a choking hazard. The play area should be free from any sharp objects, cords, or anything that could pose a danger to the baby. Electrical outlets should be covered, and furniture should be secured to the wall. The play area should be kept at a comfortable temperature, and babies should be dressed appropriately for the weather.

Encouraging movement and physical activity in babies is crucial for their healthy growth and development. You can do this by incorporating activities such as tummy time, babywearing, play gyms, and crawl tunnels. However, safety considerations should also be kept in mind during playtime to ensure the baby's safety. By following these hacks, you can encourage healthy movement and play while keeping your baby safe.

Cognitive Development

Cognitive development is an essential aspect of a baby's growth and development. It refers to the processes by which a baby acquires knowledge and understanding about the world around them. Understanding the stages of cognitive development can help you provide the right kind of stimulation to encourage your baby's growth and development.

Stage 1: Sensory Motor Stage (Birth to Two Years)

This first stage is characterized by a baby's ability to learn through their senses and motor skills. Babies at this stage learn through exploring their environment using their five senses. They also learn through actions such as grasping, reaching, and crawling.

Hack: To foster cognitive growth and development in babies at this stage, you should provide plenty of opportunities for sensory exploration. This can be done by exposing babies to a variety of stimuli such as different textures, colors, sounds, and smells. You can also encourage your baby's motor development by providing them with toys and objects that promote reaching, grasping, and crawling.

Stage 2: Preoperational Stage (Two to Eight Years)

During this stage, a baby's cognitive abilities develop rapidly, and they begin to understand symbols, language, and the world around them. They also start to develop their imagination and begin to play pretend.

Hack: To foster cognitive growth and development in babies at this stage, you should provide opportunities for exploration and imaginative play. This can be done by providing toys that allow for pretend play, such as dolls, play kitchens, and dress-up clothes. You can also encourage language development by reading books, singing songs, and engaging in conversations with your baby.

Other Stages

Stage three is the concrete operational stage (seven to 12 years) where your child begins to understand logical thinking and the concept of cause and effect. Finally, stage four is the formal operational stage (12 years and up) where your children develop abstract thinking skills and the ability to think about hypothetical situations. They also begin to think critically and make decisions based on logic and reason.

Activities To Try

Cognitive development is an essential aspect of a baby's growth and development. Understanding the different stages of cognitive development can help you provide the right kind of stimulation to encourage your baby's growth and development. By providing plenty of opportunities for sensory exploration, imaginative play, problem-solving, and critical thinking, you can encourage cognitive growth and development in your baby. Exploration and learning are crucial aspects of a baby's development. As babies grow and develop, they become more curious and interested in their surroundings, which is why it's essential to provide them with a stimulating environment that encourages new experiences. Here, we will provide tips on how to encourage exploration and learning and how to create a stimulating environment for babies.

- **Provide Opportunities for Sensory Exploration**

Babies learn about their surroundings through their senses, which is why it's essential to provide opportunities for sensory exploration. This can be done by exposing babies to different textures, colors, sounds, and smells. You can provide different toys and objects that promote sensory exploration, such as rattles, soft toys, textured balls, and musical instruments.

- **Encourage Imaginative Play**

Imaginative play is an essential aspect of a baby's development, as it helps them to develop their creativity and imagination. You can encourage imaginative play by providing toys that allow for pretend play, such as dolls, play kitchens, and dress-up clothes. You can also engage in imaginative play with your baby by playing make-believe games or storytelling.

- **Read Books and Sing Songs**

Reading books and singing songs are great ways to encourage learning and language development. Reading books to babies helps expose them to new words and concepts, while singing songs helps to develop their listening and communication skills. You can read books to your baby daily and sing songs during playtime or bedtime.

- **Provide a Variety of Toys and Objects**

Babies get bored quickly, which is why it's essential to provide them with a variety of toys and objects that promote exploration and learning. You can provide different types of toys, such as balls, stacking toys, shape sorters, and puzzles, to encourage problem-solving and fine motor skills.

Emotional and Social Development

Emotional and social development refers to a child's ability to form relationships, understand and manage emotions, and interact with others in socially appropriate ways. This development takes place throughout childhood, but some of the most critical stages occur during the early years of life.

Newborns: From birth to one month

During this stage, newborns are developing their ability to communicate through facial expressions, cries, and body movements. They are also beginning to form bonds with their caregivers.

Hacks for encouraging emotional and social development in newborns:

- Respond promptly to your baby's needs and cues. This will help them feel secure and build trust in their caregivers.
- Hold, cuddle, and talk to your baby as much as possible. This will help them feel loved and begin to form attachments with their caregivers.
- Pay attention to your baby's facial expressions and try to respond accordingly. This will help them learn how to communicate their needs and emotions.

Infancy: From one month to 12 months

During this stage, babies are developing their emotional and social skills by learning how to express themselves, form attachments, and interact with the world around them.

Hacks for fostering emotional and social development in infants:

- Provide a safe and stimulating environment for your baby to explore. This will help them learn about the world around them and develop their cognitive and motor skills.
- Encourage your baby to interact with others by introducing them to new people and engaging in play activities with them.
- Help your baby learn how to regulate their emotions by responding sensitively to their needs and providing comfort when they are upset.

Toddlerhood: From 12 months to three years

During this stage, toddlers are developing their sense of self, learning how to communicate, and beginning to understand social norms.

Hacks for promoting emotional and social development in toddlers:

- Encourage your toddler to express themselves through play, art, and other creative activities. This will help them develop their communication and self-expression skills.
- Help your toddler learn about social norms and expectations by setting clear boundaries and consequences for their behavior.
- Provide opportunities for your toddler to interact with other children, such as playdates or preschool programs. This will help them learn how to share, take turns, and cooperate with others.

Preschool years: From three years to six years

During this stage, children are developing their social skills and emotional intelligence by learning how to form friendships, regulate their emotions, and navigate social situations.

Hacks for stimulating emotional and social development in preschoolers:

- Encourage your child to participate in group activities, such as sports, clubs, or classes. This will help them learn how to cooperate with others and form friendships.
- Teach your child how to regulate their emotions by modeling healthy coping strategies and providing opportunities for them to practice these skills.
- Help your child develop empathy and understanding of others by encouraging them to consider different perspectives and supporting their efforts to help others.

Emotional Intelligence Hacks

Emotional intelligence and social skills are essential for a baby's healthy development. Emotional intelligence refers to the ability to understand, manage, and express emotions, while social skills include the ability to communicate, interact, and build relationships with others. Building emotional intelligence and social skills in babies is critical because it lays the foundation for healthy relationships, better decision-making, and effective coping with challenges later in life.

- **Respond to your baby's needs promptly**

Babies need to feel secure and loved to develop emotional intelligence and social skills. Responding promptly to their needs, such as feeding, changing, or comforting them when they are upset, helps build trust and attachment with their caregivers.

- **Engage in face-to-face interaction and play**

Babies learn social skills by engaging with others, and face-to-face interaction and play are crucial for their development. Talk to your baby, make eye contact, and smile to help them develop social skills such as communication, turn-taking, and social cues.

- **Encourage exploration and experimentation**

Babies learn about their environment through exploration and experimentation, and this helps develop their cognitive and motor skills. Encouraging exploration in a safe and stimulating environment also helps build their confidence and emotional intelligence.

- **Label and validate your baby's emotions**

Babies experience a wide range of emotions, and it's essential to label and validate them to help them develop emotional intelligence. For example, saying, "I can see you're feeling frustrated," when your baby is struggling to do something helps them understand their emotions and develop the skills to manage them.

- **Model positive social skills and emotional regulation**

Babies learn by watching and imitating their caregivers, so modeling positive social skills and emotional regulation is crucial. For example, staying calm and using a soothing tone when your baby is upset helps them learn how to manage their emotions in a positive way.

Building emotional intelligence and social skills in babies lays the foundation for healthy relationships, effective communication, and coping skills later in life. Responding promptly to their needs, engaging in face-to-face interaction and play, encouraging exploration and experimentation, labeling and validating emotions, and modeling positive social skills and emotional regulation are all practical ways to encourage these skills in your baby.

Managing Time and Energy as a Parent

Imagine a scenario where you are struggling to manage your time and energy effectively. Despite efforts to balance your work and family responsibilities, you find yourself constantly overwhelmed and stressed out. Are you scrambling to get everything done in the day? Do you wake up early to get the kids ready for the day, but still struggle to get them out of the door on time. Do you rush to work, often arriving late, and then spend your entire day dealing with work-related complaints and issues? By the time you get home in the evening, you are exhausted and just want to relax. However, you may still have to make dinner, help the kids with home-work, prepare for the next day, as well as deal with an infant baby. As a result, do you often stay up late, sacrificing sleep, which causes you to be more tired the next day?

Your inability to manage your time and money effectively might take a toll on your mental and emotional wellbeing. You might feel constantly stressed, overwhelmed, and anxious. You may also struggle to find time for self-care or to spend quality time with your loved ones. Worrying about the future may also be at the back of your mind if you cannot seem to get your schedule together. This situation is not uncommon, and it can have serious consequences for both the parent and their family. Your stress and anxiety may impact your ability to be present and attentive with your children. It is important for you to recognize when you are struggling and seek help if needed, whether it be through therapy, counseling, or other resources. By addressing these issues, you can improve their wellbeing and create a more stable environment for your children to thrive.

As a parent, taking care of yourself can sometimes feel like an impossible task. With the demands of raising children, managing a household, and potentially, balancing work, it can be challenging to find the time and energy for self-care. However, it's important to prioritize self-care to reduce stress and maintain a healthy balance. Here are some hacks for prioritizing self-care and reducing stress as a parent:

- Make self-care a priority. It's important to recognize that taking care of yourself is just as important as taking care of your children. Make self-care a priority in your daily routine, whether that means taking a few minutes to meditate, going for a walk, or taking a relaxing bath. You deserve to take care of yourself, and your children will benefit from having a happier and more relaxed parent.
- Practice mindful activities. Mindfulness is the practice of being present in the moment without

judgment. It's a powerful tool for reducing stress and increasing wellbeing. You can practice mindfulness in many ways, such as meditation, deep breathing, or simply paying attention to your thoughts and feelings without trying to change them. When you're feeling stressed or overwhelmed, take a few minutes to practice mindfulness and focus on the present moment.

- Set boundaries. As a parent, it's easy to get caught up in the demands of your children and your household. However, it's important to set boundaries to protect your time and energy. This could mean saying "no" to certain commitments or delegating tasks to others. By setting boundaries, you can ensure that you have time and energy for self-care and other important activities.

- Get enough sleep. Sleep is essential for physical and mental health, but it can be hard to come by as a parent. Make sure you're getting enough sleep by prioritizing a consistent bedtime routine, creating a comfortable sleep environment, and limiting screen time before bed. If you're having trouble sleeping, consider talking to your doctor or a sleep specialist.

- Practice self-compassion. Parenting can be challenging, and it's easy to be hard on yourself when things don't go as planned. However, practicing self-compassion can help you reduce stress and maintain a healthy perspective. Treat yourself with kindness and understanding, just as you would a close friend. Remember that you're doing the best you can, and that it's okay to make mistakes.

- Connect with others. Parenting can be isolating, especially if you're a stay-at-home parent or if your children are very young. It's important to connect with others to reduce stress and maintain a sense of community. This could mean joining a parent group, attending playdates, or simply reaching out to friends or family members for support.

- Prioritize physical activity. Exercise is a powerful tool for reducing stress and improving overall health. As a parent, it can be challenging to find time for exercise, but it's important to prioritize physical activity. This could mean going for a walk with your children, practicing yoga at home, or joining a gym with childcare.

- Seek professional help if needed. If you're feeling overwhelmed or are struggling with mental health issues, don't hesitate to seek professional help. A therapist or counselor can provide you with the support and tools you need to manage stress and maintain a healthy balance.

Maintaining a healthy balance as a parent can be challenging, but it's essential for your wellbeing and the wellbeing of your family. By prioritizing self-care, you can reduce stress and maintain a healthy balance as a parent. Remember that taking care of yourself is not selfish—it's essential for being the best parent you can be.

Your Love Life

Keeping a strong relationship going with your partner can be challenging when you have young children. The demands of parenthood can leave little time and energy for romance and intimacy. However, there are many activities parents can do to keep their relationship alive while having young children. Schedule regular date nights with your partner, even if it's just a simple dinner or a movie at home after the kids have gone to bed. Make it a priority to spend time alone with your partner without the distractions of children or other responsibilities. Small romantic gestures can go a long way in keeping your relationship alive. This could be as simple as leaving a love note or sending a thoughtful text message during the day. Show your partner that you appreciate and value them.

Find a shared hobby or interest that you can enjoy together, whether it's cooking, hiking, or watching a favorite TV show. This can help you bond and strengthen your relationship. Physical intimacy is an important part of a romantic relationship. Even if you're exhausted from parenting, try to make time for physical intimacy with your partner. This could mean setting aside time for sex or simply cuddling and holding hands. Effective communication is essential for a strong relationship. Make sure you're taking time to talk to your partner and share your thoughts and feelings. This can help you work through any issues or conflicts that arise and strengthen your connection.

Parenthood can be stressful and overwhelming. Make sure you're supporting each other as parents and as partners. Show your partner that you're there for them and be willing to help out with childcare and household tasks when needed. Taking care of yourself is important for your own wellbeing and for your relationship. Make sure you're taking time for self-care and pursuing your own interests and hobbies. This can help you feel more fulfilled and energized in your relationship. Remember that keeping your relationship alive while having young children takes effort and intentionality. By making extra effort, you can maintain a strong and fulfilling relationship with your partner.

Fostering Physical and Cognitive Development Through Playtime

Playtime is essential for the physical, social, and cognitive development of children. Playtime allows children to explore their surroundings, develop their creativity, build physical skills, and learn important social skills. Playtime helps children develop their gross and fine motor skills. For example, running, jumping, and climbing help develop gross motor skills, while playing with puzzles and building blocks help develop fine motor skills. Playtime also helps children develop their cognitive skills. Through play, children learn problem-solving, decision-making, and critical thinking skills. They also develop their language and communication skills.

Playtime provides children with opportunities to interact with others and develop social skills such as cooperation, negotiation, and conflict resolution. Consider your child's age and developmental level when choosing playtime activities. For example, toddlers may enjoy playing with blocks, while older children may prefer board games or puzzles. Children are more likely to engage in playtime activities that are fun and enjoyable. Make sure the activities you choose are interactive and engaging. Toys and games can be a great way to make playtime more educational. Look for toys and games that promote problem-solving, creativity, and critical thinking.

Physical activity is important for children's physical development. Encourage your child to engage in physical activities such as running, jumping, and climbing. Unstructured play allows children to use their imagination and creativity. Allow your child to play freely and explore their environment. Playing with your child can be a great way to bond and promote their development. Join in on the playtime activities and encourage your child to ask questions and explore their surroundings. Through play, babies learn about their environment, develop social skills, and build physical strength and coordination.

- Playtime should begin early in a baby's life. Even newborns can benefit from simple sensory play experiences, such as being exposed to different textures, colors, and sounds.
- Offer a variety of experiences. Babies need a variety of play experiences to promote healthy growth and development. Offer experiences that promote sensory exploration, physical activity, and social interaction.
- Follow your baby's lead. Babies have their own unique personalities and preferences. Follow your baby's lead during playtime and encourage exploration of their interests.
- Be present and engaged. During playtime, be present and engaged with your baby. Offer encouragement, praise, and positive reinforcement to help build their confidence and self-esteem.
- Allow for unstructured play. Unstructured playtime allows babies to use their imagination and creativity. Allow your baby to play freely and explore their environment without too many rules or limitations.

Overall, play is an essential aspect of a baby's healthy growth and development. By providing a safe and stimulating play environment, following your baby's lead, and offering a variety of experiences, you can promote your baby's learning and development in fun and engaging ways.

Encouraging Bonding and Playtime with Your Baby

The lack of bonding with a baby can have significant consequences for their emotional, cognitive, and social development. A child who does not bond adequately with their
parents may have difficulty regulating their emotions and may
be more prone to anxiety, depression, and other mental health
issues. Bonding is a critical component of attachment, which
refers to the emotional connection between a child and their
primary caregiver. A child who does not bond adequately may
struggle to form healthy attachments with others later in life.
Bonding and attachment are also essential for cognitive development, as they help children learn about the world around
them and develop their language and problem-solving skills.
Babies and children who do not bond adequately may be at
risk for cognitive delays and learning difficulties.

A child who does not bond adequately may have difficulty
forming relationships with peers and may struggle with social
skills later in life. Babies who do not receive adequate bonding
and nurturing may experience chronic stress, which can have
long-term health consequences. It's important to note that
bonding is a two-way process, and parents who struggle to
bond with their baby may also experience feelings of anxiety,
depression, and other mental health issues. Seeking support
and guidance from healthcare professionals, family, and
friends can be helpful in building a stronger bond with your
baby. Bonding with a new baby is essential for their emotional
and cognitive development, and it is also an incredible opportunity for parents to create a deep and loving connection with
their child.

Gently massaging your baby can help them relax and improve
their digestion. Use a natural oil, like coconut or olive oil, and

gently massage your baby's arms, legs, and tummy. Reading to your baby can help stimulate their brain development and language skills. Choose simple picture books with bright colors and simple words, and read to your baby in a gentle, soothing tone. There are some activities that the whole family can partake in to bond with the new baby such as:

- Take a family walk with the baby in a stroller or carrier. This can be a great opportunity to get some fresh air and exercise and also bond with your baby as you point out different sights and sounds.
- Enjoying meals together as a family is a great way to bond with your baby. Even if the baby isn't old enough to eat solid food yet, they can still sit at the table with you and enjoy the company.
- When the baby is a little older, incorporate them into family game night. Choose age-appropriate games and activities that everyone can participate in.
- Plan outings that the whole family can enjoy together, like a trip to the park, zoo, or museum. These experiences can create lasting memories and strengthen family bonds.
- Watching a movie together as a family can be a fun and relaxing way to bond with your baby. Choose a family-friendly movie and snuggle up together on the couch.

Overall, the key to bonding with a new baby is to be present and engaged in their world. Spend time with them, talk to them, and respond to their needs with love and patience. By doing so, you'll create a strong and lasting bond that will benefit both you and your baby for years to come.

Every child is different. It is crucial to consider these differences while observing your baby's growth and development. Witnessing your baby's progress through various stages during their first year of life is an exciting experience. Every milestone, from their first steps to their first meal, feels like a significant achievement worth commemorating. As you observe your little one's growth, you become amazed by their newfound abilities and intrigued by what they will do next. The anticipation of their first words, their first day at nursery school, and other enchanting moments that come with each developmental stage heighten the excitement. It's a thrilling journey that you share with your child, and the joy and fascination of it all makes every challenging moment and sleepless night worthwhile.

Chapter 4
Creative Baby Hacks

Here comes the "fun" part where we discuss the baby hacks that save you money. Creating your own products to use when bathing, changing, feeding, entertaining, and teaching your baby will save you hundreds of dollars annually. If you are able to acquire the necessary ingredients for these revolutionary items, you and your baby will be much happier in the long run. A happy household equals a happy child!

Most of the time, you can reuse everyday items you have around your home already! Upcycle that broken-handled pot and give your tiny tot a wooden spoon so they can become the next stellar drummer. Reuse an empty tissue box to turn it into a guitar by wrapping four rubber bands around the opening for easy strumming. Get the most out of any broken crayons your toddler snaps while trying out their pincer grasp by melting the broken crayon pieces in an oven-safe mold to make your own rainbow-inspired jumbo crayons. Set the oven to 275 °F. Pour warm tap water in a large bowl and let the crayons soak for 5-10 minutes to peel off the paper wrapper while your oven preheats. Place the now naked crayons into the oven-safe mold, place the mold onto a baking sheet, and let melt for 35 minutes. Voila! New crayons, like magic!

Saving Money on Baby Products

With so many products on grocery store shelves marketed toward people who care for babies, toddlers, and children of all ages, it can be challenging to choose the right product for your budget and what you need it to do. If you're spending an exponential amount of money on a certain baby body wash because it's the most expensive and (possibly) the "best" for your baby's delicate skin, you will likely be able to find a much less costly substitute that contains the exact same ingredients if you choose a store brand rather than a brand-name product.

If you can take the time in the store to read the ingredients label that is usually located on the back of the product, compare ingredients between your preferred product and an off-brand or store brand product that has a similar formula. You will save dollars doing this that will add up quickly.

Do this with cereals and snacks that your child devours by the handful. They will likely not notice a difference in taste, but you will begin to see the financial benefit of choosing a cheaper product because you'll be saving so much more at the store.

Another great way to save on expensive items that your child will probably not use very long is to shop second-hand. Consignment stores, yard sales, online or social media groups, and asking friends and family members for hand-me-down clothes, highchairs, and large toys like exersaucers will also save you hundreds of dollars.

If you look at the few weeks your child will use these objects or clothes relative to how much you pay for them brand new, you will find the two do not balance. So, don't break the bank trying to entertain or clothe your child. They will grow out of each of these more quickly than you can replenish the funds in savings.

Budgeting for Larger Purchases

When you need an item new, not used, for any number of reasons, the best thing you can do is to start saving months in advance. A general rule of thumb for how to realistically accomplish this is to start small while taking care of your family's day-to-day expenses.

First, you will want to assign 50% of your monthly, weekly, or yearly income to your family's needs like car payments, utilities, housing payment, groceries, gas, and car and health insurance. These are your first priority, too, if you find yourself in financial trouble. These are the bills your family cannot afford to ignore. Then, you can allocate 30% of your income to things that you want. This includes entertainment, hobbies or interests, and dining out as well as any family vacations you plan to take together.

Lastly, the remaining 20% will go to savings. Here you will store and find the financial resources you will need when making larger purchases. The balance in your savings account should increase significantly with each passing paycheck. Before long, you will have accumulated enough money to purchase a new car seat, crib, or toddler bed of your dreams.

If you need an item now and have no savings to speak of, keep calm and parent on! You can make due with using a pack-n-play as a crib for a couple weeks until you can afford a toddler bed if you absolutely need to. One of the beauties of parenthood is learning to adapt to adverse situations because you never know when something unexpected will pop up. Just make sure there are no holes, tears, or gaps in the play yard, and you have a safe alternative where your baby can sleep safely no matter where you go.

Making Your Own Baby Products

Making baby foods, infant-safe cleaning products, and baby body wash has a plethora of advantages. You can customize each product to meet your child's personal needs. If they have a skin allergy or you need a tear-free version of your own body wash or skincare product, you are able to make one safely in the comfort of your own home without breaking the bank.

There are also numerous ways to prepare your own baby foods by using a blender or food processor. Just add broth (chicken, beef, or vegetable) to any cooked vegetable, like peas or carrots, and mash them together. You've made a healthy alternative to store-bought, high processed baby's first foods. You could also smash cooked veggies with a fork or cut banana slices into quarters so that your little one can learn to enjoy foods that you eat, too.

Food preparation, food choices, and family meals are a wonderful way to introduce your child to your family traditions and cultural inheritance. There may be generations worth of recipes that are easily adaptable for children that have been passed down through members of your family to you. It is never too early, or too late, to help your little one appreciate their roots through the foods you choose to prepare for them.

Remain close to your child during mealtimes so that if they experience challenges with chewing, you are able to intervene quickly. Most of the time, your child will benefit from coughing to get the food back up on their own without intervention. Sometimes, panicking, smacking the child on the back, and forcing your fingers into their mouth to retrieve any obstruction will push the food further into their throat. The best thing you can do is watch carefully for signs that your child cannot cough up the bit of food independently, and only jump in when you see that they are beginning to struggle.

This is, of course, a rare emergency that will most likely not occur, but you will want to be prepared for those just-in-case situations as your child is learning to eat solids. Start with the most watered-down version of the foods you prepare, then you will want to work up to soft chunks that are smaller than your fingernail. Once your child is around nine months old and able to sit on their own, you can introduce finger foods, like Cheerios, which double as a perfect way to strengthen their pincer grasp. They will need this fine motor skill as they learn to write or hold a crayon on their own and button up their jacket independently.

To ensure your child eats a well-balanced meal, you can offer foods that you prepare for the entire family as long as they are small enough (smaller than your fingernail) and are soft enough for children who may not have all their teeth in yet to chew food thoroughly. This way, you introduce your child to foods specific to your family, and they are included in family meals. You also save an incredible amount of money by not purchasing additional foods that are marketed at an increased price just because they are "for babies." It's a win-win for everyone.

Diaper Cream Recipe

Invest in smaller glass jars to store homemade baby oil and diaper rash cream for fast, easy, all-natural skin-soothing recipes. For a baby with blisters on their bottom, a safe remedy is to dilute five drops of tea tree oil with two tablespoons of jojoba or coconut oil before placing the mixture directly on the affected area. This concoction also works to help heal impetigo or other bacterial skin infections naturally. Applying tea tree oil directly to the skin is ill-advised because it will cause a burning sensation on irritated skin.

For this multi-purpose salve, you will need to acquire tallow, olive oil, and an appropriate essential oil of your choice. An infant-safe list of essential oils you can use for this recipe are:

- Bergamot (five drops bergamot diluted by four tablespoons carrier oil)
- Catnip
- Chamomile
- Clary sage
- Dill weed (seven drops dill weed diluted by two tablespoons carrier oil)
- Lavender
- Lemon (twelve drops lemon diluted by two tablespoons carrier oil)
- Lime
- Mandarin
- Neroli
- Orange
- Rose (fifteen drops rose diluted by two tablespoons carrier oil)
- Spearmint (ten drops spearmint diluted by two tablespoons carrier oil)
- Tea tree
- Vanilla

Many of the citrus-related essential oils mentioned above are best used during the day, as they provide a burst of energy. Use lavender, chamomile, catnip, neroli, rose, and catnip at night for a calming effect before bed.

You will need the following and a 4-ounce glass jar with a lid to store the salve in afterwards. It will yield ½ cup, or four ounces:

- 27 drops essential oils chosen from the baby-safe list above if the salve is going to be applied to the face, a sunburn, eczema, or other boo-boo; use only 8 drops if this recipe will be used as a diaper ointment for a child under the age of two
- 2 tablespoons olive oil
- 3 ½ ounces tallow, or ½ cup melted tallow

In a medium saucepan over low heat, add the tallow and stir until melted. Use a large bowl to combine the now liquid tallow, olive oil, and drops of essential oils. Let the mixture rest for one hour before using a hand mixer to whip the concoction until fluffy like the consistency of cake frosting. DO NOT INGEST! Once whipped, store the balm in a sterile jar and store in a cool, dry location for up to one year. Apply as often as needed to rehydrate and protect chapped, delicate skin.

Organic Teething Ointment

This recipe is safe to use for babies who are going through the growing pains of getting in their milk teeth. It can be a pain! And not just for your child, but for you as well. Soothe your little one's gums, and your nerves, by preparing this edible remedy and rubbing a few drops of it directly on your baby's gums up to four times a day.

- 12 drops clove essential oil (food grade) OR 1 tablespoon whole cloves
- ¼ cup cocoa butter (pure food grade)
- ¼ cup olive oil OR coconut oil

In a medium saucepan over low heat, mix the coconut (or olive oil) with the cocoa butter. Pour in the cloves (or clove essential oil) and turn off the heat to allow the mixture time to heat. This will take about 20-30 minutes. Do not allow the mixture to solidify, as you will want to sieve out the cloves through a fine mesh strainer or several layers of cheesecloth draped over a small glass jar that has a lid for storage. At room temperature, the mixture will remain in a liquid state. In the refrigerator, you will have a more solid product. Rest assured; this natural pain-relief remedy is safe for your baby to ingest at low doses.

Simplifying Baby-Related Chores

Bath Time

You could opt for the "fast bath" method where you run some warm water, gently toss your tot "into the drink", and scrub what needs to be scrubbed before rinsing off the suds, or you could make bath time an educational opportunity to bond with your little one. Children always learn more, and these lessons are remembered better, when they involve some element of fun. Whether you choose an extended bath time to learn cause and effect though pouring water from various cup sizes or pick the fast bath, ensure you spend quality time with your child because they won't always be this little.

Bath time can be a messy aqua escapade that leaves your bathroom a wet, moldy mess. Bring in the box fan or wet vac to help dry the room if your bathroom lacks a vent system or window you can open once your little seahorses have finished dressing. Sop up any excess water on the floor with the towel you used to dry your child off and then hang it from the shower curtain rod to dry before adding it to your laundry pile to help reduce the risk of growing mold. Mildew and mold love moist darkness so prevent the growth of these hazardous fungi by ensuring any laundry items go into the hamper dry or launder them right away (if you have the time for that).

For this same reason (mold is not our friend!) you will need to check any toys your child plays with in the tub weekly for signs of black mold. Yellow duckies will become a duller yellow as the inside of these squirt toys fills with black mold, even if you squirt out all the water after each use. So, replace them as soon as you notice deterioration and discoloration.

Foam letters and numbers can be cut from large foam pieces or purchased at a low cost. These will stick to the sides of the tub when wet. Your little ones can learn colors, shapes, letters, numbers, and words quickly and enjoyably by using this bath toy. They're also less prone to becoming moldy because they have no holes and dry quickly!

Make quick work of bath time and get the scrubbing out of the way first. Use a clean, wet washcloth without soap to clean your baby's eyes, ears, nose, and face first. Then you'll want to wash their hair. Keep a large, empty cup in with their bath supplies so that you can easily rinse the suds away from their delicate eyes. Even the no-tears stuff still stings.

Teach your child to tilt their head back to encourage the water to run down their back instead of into their face. Then, you can wash the rest of their body and let them play until the water runs out of the tub. It's a win-win for everyone.

Bath-Time Baby Body Wash Recipe

Mix in a tablespoon of your own mild body wash with three parts aloe vera (you can also use sunburn aftercare salve made from aloe vera) to save money, keep your baby's skin soft, and reduce the need to buy so many different products at the store for self-care. You only need about a quarter-size amount on a soft washcloth before each bath time to adequately clean your child.

Here's a pro-tip if your child is suffering from a yeast infection diaper rash: Pour in one cup of apple cider vinegar to your child's bath water each night to help soothe and treat these kinds of rashes caused by yeast growth. Apply a protective ointment to your child's rash once they are thoroughly dry after their bath. One amazing product—A & D ointment, not the cream—contains lanolin that will lessen the sting from having a diaper rash while it also nourishes and acts as a moisture barrier to protect this incredibly delicate skin as it heals.

A more natural, but probably more expensive, alternative to the baby-safe body wash listed above is to purchase a bottle of Pure Castile Soap, a bottle of vegetable glycerin, a bottle of almond or jojoba oil (to be the carrier oil for this recipe), a small bottle of lavender essential oil to induce sleepy-time feelings before bed, and aloe vera gel along with a 16-ounce glass jar with a pump bottle top to store this mixture in.

Incorporate all ingredients in the glass jar as follows:

- 1-2 tablespoons distilled or filtered water
- 1-2 teaspoons of jojoba oil, almond oil, OR appropriate carrier oil you prefer
- 1 tablespoon lavender essential oil
- ¼ cup vegetable glycerin

- 1 ½ cups liquid, unscented pure Castile soap
- 1 teaspoon aloe vera gel (optional)

Place the lid onto the jar securely and then shake the jar until all ingredients are well-incorporated. This mixture is usable for up to two weeks. The storage time is three to six months longer if you do not add water to the mixture. Increase the amount of vegetable glycerin used if you wish for more bubbles in the lather. Use ½ a cup of vegetable glycerin instead of ¼ cup if you desire more suds.

Bedtime

Bedtime can be a nightmare for parents. It's honestly probably not much fun for babies and toddlers, either. They are always ready to explore their environment and might fear missing something important. Maybe they aren't ready to say "good-night" just yet, but you are, and sleep is imperative to help little bodies and brains grow. The main purpose of the sleep cycle is to help the body rejuvenate and repair. It has a difficult time doing this when all systems are "go", so the brain shuts down excess functions to focus the needed energy for repairs and cell growth.

Maybe you've found a song your child gravitates to for nap time; perhaps Taylor Swift is your child's chosen lullaby, but whatever it is, if it soothes your child to sleep, go for it. Disregard any strange looks from strangers who might judge you in public because you are the only person who gets to make choices for your child (even any poor tastes in music), so ignore everyone else. Focus on your child. Sing their lullaby anywhere and everywhere when they are fussy. Make it fun: If you're in the checkout line at the grocery store or waiting patiently for a restroom stall to open up, sing whatever songs are going to get them to calm down.

Your calm will compensate for their "crazy." They will begin to feel your soothing presence takeover as you sing, or read a bedtime story, or whatever calming ritual you find works for your little one. Keep doing it. Kids thrive on routine, when certain events happen in the same way they can count on every day.

Maybe you will give your child a bath after dinner, then read a book as they snuggle in bed with their favorite toy or blanket. Dimming the light throughout the rest of the house will help their minds recognize that it's time to wind down.

Taking Care of Your Baby's Feet

Once your little one starts walking, everything becomes a toy to them. It's a novel game to grab anything within reach and as fast as they learned to walk, all of a sudden, now they're running! Now that your baby is using their feet for something other than being an adorable receptacle for your kisses of adoration, you'll need to protect those piggies!

Shoes at this stage should be an affordable, sturdy material that supports the developing arch of your child's foot and stabilizes the developing ankle muscles to keep your child steady on their feet. Buying shoes that are too big in hopes that your child will grow into them is not feasible. It's also a dangerous tripping hazard for your child.

They'll scuff and wear out their shoes before they ever grow into their shoes at this stage because their growth rate is its most rapid during the first five years. Your child will experience another time of high velocity growth during adolescence when they go through puberty. That's a whole other convoluted topic with its own challenges enough for another book. You'll be buying a lot of new shoes then, too.

Try not to fret about the future. Buy shoes that fit your child now. You will get the best fit if you have your child stand up straight while wearing both shoes, feet together. Then, take your thumb and press it to find your child's big toe through the fabric of each shoe. You should feel about a half-inch of space between the tip of your child's toe and the end of the shoe. There should be no gaps between your child's heel and the back of the shoe so watch them when they walk around the shoe aisle before you purchase them.

Keep the receipt and shoe box for at least a week after bringing the new shoes home. If you find out later that the shoes are uncomfortable for your child, for whatever reason, or the shoes just do not work, you can always return them for another pair or exchange them for a different size.

Seek store brands that are more affordable during those growth spurts. They're usually under $20, sturdy, and will wear well compared to name brands that cost upwards of $50 for something your child will not be wearing for more than a few weeks, at most.

Other dad-hacks to helping protect your precious ones' piggies is to take a look at their socks, especially if your baby is fussy and you've tried everything else to soothe them. Their diaper is clean, their tummy is full, and you've been walking and holding your little one close for a long time, but nothing seems to help quiet your baby's cries. It could be their socks or footwear.

Check your child's toes (and fingers) frequently for stray strings or even long hairs wrapped around these tiny digits. They can be easy to miss and it's not something you may think about, but thread comes loose all the time inside infant socks (I don't know why!) but your baby's toes can become entangled or otherwise made uncomfortable by these manufacturing flaws. You can cut the loose strings inside the socks before placing them on your child's foot or discard them when they begin to unravel.

You'll probably lose a lot of socks as your baby kicks them off or the dryer eats them, so prepare to invest in several pairs in varying sizes. You can also turn your baby's socks inside out to avoid threads altogether. Just make sure that, no matter how you orient the socks, they are the right size and not too small.

Accessing High-Quality Baby Items for Less

Consignment shops are now your best friend. Unless you have a best friend who had a new baby just before your little one made their appearance and they are willing to part with their gently-used, like-new baby items, like a changing table, stroller, breast pump, crib, sling, or other items. Since baby- and toddler-hood do not last very long in terms of months of daily use versus how costly the item is, it is well-advised to find secondhand items.

You may need to go the extra steps to thoroughly sterilize anything that has been used before, but if the price is right— typically a third of the original cost—the price is much more affordable relative to how short a time your child will actually use the toy or larger purchase because they grow out of things so quickly.

You may check online for social media groups that post gently-used items you need or want. Other options are to ask family, friends, and coworkers if anyone knows where to purchase something larger like a car seat or highchair.

Used car seats can be a tricky item to acquire because if you do not know the previous owner, you cannot ask if the car seat was ever in a vehicle that was involved in an accident. You never want to pick up or use a car seat that is damaged in any way. The reliability of the protection it provides your child in the event of a car crash is severely compromised if the seat is not up to standard. So, only purchase a verified car seat that states it has not been in an accident, one that is new in its box, or one from a person you trust.

Always check for an expiration date on your child's car seat. This date is usually printed on the underside, side, or back of the car seat. It may seem silly that a non-food object has an expiration date, but the materials used to manufacture baby products do not always withstand the test of time or damage sustained through normal wear and tear. Children are always tough on the items they use, no matter how careful they try to be. It's a fact of life, and nothing lasts forever. So, it is best to replace a car seat that has been used as soon as you notice the expiration date is about to pass. This way, you will keep your little one safe and gain the peace of mind that the car seat protecting your child in the event of a car accident is at its optimal level of functionality.

Chapter 5
The Toddler Years and Building on Baby Hacks

Congratulations on a job well done! You're almost done with diapers; you've endured those zombie nights of no sleep. Now that your not-so-helpless little wonder begins to wander, you need to invest in better baby-proofing by way of thick, plastic corner protectors for coffee tables and other low-lying furniture. You'll notice your baby may bruise easily on their foreheads and legs. This is because they are clumsy and rarely look up before their brow connects with the kitchen table or bookcase.

Have no fear and try to not feel bad for your baby's bruises as they explore their environment. These innocuous bumps and bruises are part of normal development and will fade with time.

For those difficult-to-break-through molars and incisors, invest in teething rings you can freeze and paper towels to wrap around these life-saving products whenever you need to apply ice to your baby's boo-boos or swollen gums. There is little you can do to prevent these kinds of injuries or ailments, but you can lessen the amount of pain these hazards cause by applying ice to the affected area, never heat.

If store-bought baby-proofing items prove too expensive, there are still safe alternatives you can "hack" at home. Follow along below for ways to entertain, teach, protect, and keep your child happy, healthy, and whole into their toddler years.

Introduction to Baby-Proofing: The Toddler Years

There are two magic words that can solve several of your baby-proofing dilemmas and it usually costs below $10: Duct tape! You can choose any color or pattern, but the silver stuff works wonders on its own. Need to keep the refrigerator door closed from would-be mess-makers? No problem, a sliver of the silver stuff is all you need to keep the door closed. Apply a small strip out of your child's reach (or higher if your child has learned to move a chair to climb on), and they can struggle for hours to access the contents while you giggle at their adorableness.

Duct tape is easily removable by adept, adult hands. Any residue the adhesive leaves behind can be erased by using a little rubbing alcohol on a paper towel.

Get creative with this quick-fix gadget by investing in tape with patterns. Layer triangle-cut-out slices of the duct tape to completely cover each corner of your coffee table. Note that using duct tape on fireplace fixtures is not recommended because of the possibility the polymer will melt if the fireplace is in use. Splurge and get the fire-resistant childproofing product, here.

Duct tape is also a fairly fun item for your toddler to play with that will help develop small motor skill finger dexterity. Just always be cautious that your little darlings don't put it in their mouths. Anything that fits through the tube of a toilet paper roll can be a choking hazard.

Advanced Parenting Hacks

Children of all ages thrive on routine, consistency, and stability. To know that you will react, and the world around them will produce the same result if they perform a certain action every time, then their minds will commit to memory the cause and effect. This builds confidence for the child who knows to expect a time out if they hit their sibling. This also teaches children that gravity will cause an object to fall no matter how it was dropped or thrown. And if they misbehave in public, they know to anticipate not getting dessert after dinner.

One parenting hack for a child who refuses to leave the playground is to call out a five-minute warning to alert your child it's almost time to leave. This helps them understand a transition is coming between playing and going home. If your little one begins to balk at a two-minute warning, get on their level to look them in the eyes for assurance they are paying attention to you and calmly, but firmly, say, "We're going home. You can slide one more time but we're leaving after that."

You shouldn't have to carry your child, kicking and screaming, from the playground. This isn't healthy for you (or your back) or for your child. If they refuse to walk with you to the car to go home, and you resort to physically removing them from the playground, once your child and you are settled in your car, seat belts on, turn to your child and explain that "We will visit the park another day. I know you were having fun, and that's good, but it's not okay to make me carry you. It hurts me. We can go to the park again next week, and if we leave the park without crying, we can have your favorite snack (or activity) when we get home."

It's important to set realistic boundaries, limitations, and expectations for your child. Speak to them like they are capable of understanding everything you say because they are. Even if they are nonverbal, your child will grasp the concept of what you're explaining to them, and this makes them more likely to comply in the future. Keep consequences consistent and sentences simplistic. Your child will thrive when they know what to expect from you.

Playtime and Learning

Your child benefits greatly from structured play as well as independent, child-directed playtime. A child's cognitive abilities develop more rapidly when they are encouraged to use their imagination in purposeful play like using a toy kitchen to make pretend meals. This is how children mimic what they see adults do. Provide them with these tools if you can afford to do so by shopping at yard sales and secondhand stores instead of paying full price for brand new items.

If you've recently upgraded your phone and you have an old model that you don't need to keep charged anymore, you might consider giving this item to your child to play with so they can practice their communication skills. Turn-taking in conversations can be taught as you pretend to talk on your phone to them through their discontinued phone. You may also choose to give discarded remote controls (with the batteries removed), pots and pans, and other realistic objects that kids gravitate towards anyway instead of buying the toy version.

Help your child develop their emotional awareness, too, by helping your child "care" for their stuffed animals. You may choose to purchase a pretend doctor's kit, or you could use a few Band-Aids from your well-stocked first aid kit to patch up a stuffed bear's scuffed knee so that your child begins to understand the concept of empathy and caring for others.

Most toddlers and young children are self-centered in that they are born innocently believing their feelings, thoughts, and are shared by everyone. This is part of nature's design for self-preservation: A newborn must act in instinctual ways that will ensure their needs are met first. This is evidenced by how often newborn babies cry to alert a caretaker to assist the child because they are unable to do so by themselves. They have not yet developed the capacity to understand that each person exists independently from themselves and that their actions have consequences. They might understand that their friend hurt their feelings but not realize that they have the ability to hurt their friend's feelings, too.

The ability to empathize with others will develop around age four (Kutner, 2016).

According to researchers Palanikumar Balasundaram and Indirapriya Darshini Avulakunta, "the best predictor of cognitive function is language" (2023). This means that a typically-developing toddler will be able to respond to their name when called, be able to answer questions when asked, and use more than three-word-sentences. Toddlers are categorized as children who are between ages one and three.

During this time, language and speech development should be developed enough that your child uses around 50 distinct words to describe everyday items and activities that your family uses. You may notice that your child is advanced in certain areas, such as being proficient climbers and problem solvers, when it comes to using their large motor skills, or they may be blossoming Picasso's holding their paintbrush and pencils correctly while drawing their masterpieces.

Children develop a myriad of skills at their own pace. While certain areas of development (physical, emotional, social, cognitive, language and communication, and motor function) may develop more rapidly or more proficiently, some areas of development will surpass others as your child takes turns developing their skill set. Not all areas of development progress at equal rates.

Areas that seem to be lacking will catch up over time. Helping your child strengthen their areas of weakness (without explicitly calling attention to these deficits to your child) will allow them the opportunity to strengthen these skills and your child will benefit, too, from extra play time with you.

First Aid Tips and Tricks

Always carry a small pouch inside your diaper bag or purse filled with antibiotic ointment, Band-Aids, antihistamine cream and chewables, tissues, and wipes so that you can tend to any first aid issue that arises. You never know when a cut, scrape, or bloody nose will occur. It's best to be prepared for anything.

Applying pressure to wounds will help provide a barrier so that blood cannot escape easily; this encourages coagulation so that the body can begin to form a scab and the blood stops flowing. You may need to apply direct pressure for up to two minutes before the blood begins to slow enough to clean the area, apply antibiotic ointment, and put on a Band-Aid big enough to cover the entire wound. If the wound is deeper or wider than two inches, you should take your child to the emergency room or urgent care for stitches.

Give your child a bath and remove the Band-Aid while wet to decrease the pain of removing the adhesive from dry skin.

Gently clean the wound with a wet, soapy washcloth and run water over it until the suds are gone. You do not need stringent antiseptics like rubbing alcohol or hydrogen peroxide to clean a wound. These will break down healthy cells that promote healing. Warm, clean water and soap are all you need for proper wound care.

Once your child is dry, apply a fresh Band-Aid with antibiotic ointment (this will also reduce scarring) so that the wound doesn't become infected. Whenever possible over the next few days, remove the bandage and only cover the wound with a thin layer of antibiotic ointment so that oxygen can help the wound heal. If you're going to the playground or somewhere where the wound could get debris or germs, you should cover the cut with a Band-Aid before you leave the house.

Nosebleeds

For nosebleeds that seem like a never-ending gush, you should keep your child's head tilted toward their feet to allow the blood to drain out rather than back down their throat. Swallowing the blood in this way will make your child feel nauseous. If you can, apply an ice poultice or cold compress to the bridge of the nose and hold pressure with a bunch of tissues to stave the blood loss. Get crafty here and use a baggie full of ice cubes with a paper towel wrapped around it so the skin is protected from frostbite. Use a bag of frozen peas over the nose or wrap a frozen teething ring in a thin tea towel. Anything cold will do so long as you gently pinch the nose and lean your child slightly forward. All you can really do in this instance is wait until the bleeding stops. Clean up your child's face and encourage them to take it easy for the next hour so that the bleeding doesn't start again.

Easier said than done? Maybe you could put them in their stroller and take a walk with them so that they stay elevated and still. Another suggestion would be to give your child a popsicle and have them watch a 30-minute TV program they enjoy or go for a short, scenic drive with your little one.

Allergy, Rash, Bites, and Stings

For bee stings, poison ivy rash, or food allergy on the go, you should stock your first aid kit with some kind of antihistamine cream and chewable tablets. If your child's allergy is severe and starts to go into anaphylactic shock, take your child to the nearest emergency room immediately and call 911 on the way. Symptoms to look for that this kind of allergic reaction is severe are difficulty breathing, swelling of the face, tongue, and hands, and wheezing as if the airway is constricting.

Less severe allergic reactions will be swelling isolated to the insect bite or sting, itchy rash that looks like hives, sneezing, coughing, runny nose, and eye redness. Seasonal allergies can be controlled with medications like Zyrtec, Claritin, or Allegra. Consuming local, raw honey (once your child is over the age of two to reduce the risk of botulism spores causing a worse illness) will further help strengthen your child's resistance to local pollen because bees and other pollinators are taking nearby allergens (pollen) and turning them into honey. Items that use honey are okay as long as the honey has been baked like in cereals and graham crackers.

If your child is stung by a bee and the stinger is still present, use a credit card to gently scrape across the skin to loosen the stinger. You can also use tweezers or sharp fingernails to pluck the stinger out. The longer you leave the stinger in, the more venom is pumped into the wound, so you'll want to remove it immediately. Apply a cold compress, if you can, to reduce swelling and the burning pain. Distract your child as best you can to keep them calm.

It can take up to two hours after the initial sting for an allergic reaction to appear (*How long does it take to have an allergic reaction to a bee sting?*, 2021). The best thing you can do is watch your child carefully for signs of trouble breathing or swallowing up to five hours after the incident. Hives will likely appear on the skin as red, itchy welts. Your child may complain that their head hurts. If your child is nonverbal, they may be more fussy or irritable. Fainting, vomiting, drowsiness, or difficulty paying attention to you or responding to their name are signs you should take your child to the emergency room without delay.

Poison Ivy, Poison Oak, and Poison Sumac

The best way to ward off those itchy rashes caused when your skin comes into contact with poison ivy, poison oak, and poison sumac is to wash the exposed area with dish detergent that contains a degreaser in the ingredients list on the back of the product label. These plants produce an oily substance called "urushiol" that can be washed off before it causes skin irritation and rash, but if you are unable to wash the area immediately, you can clean up with a baby wipe. Refrain from scratching because this will spread the irritant further and increase the affected area.

If you notice a raised red rash around your little one's eyes, nose, and mouth, you will need to take them to the emergency room (ER) or urgent care. This kind of allergic reaction is dangerous and could restrict their nasal passages, cause swelling of the esophagus, and decrease your child's ability to breathe or swallow. If the rash spreads to the genitals, this situation also calls for a trip to the ER, doctor, or urgent care because the skin is so thin in this area and could cause further complications. A rash in this area also indicates a severe allergic reaction that needs to be monitored by a doctor.

Calamine lotion, Benadryl, or other hydrocortisone creams can be applied topically directly to the freshly washed and gently dried itchy rash. Encourage your little one to keep from scratching by placing a bag of frozen vegetables over the itchy area if possible. The ice will abate the intense itch that causes your child to want to scratch. Keep your child's nails short by trimming them with nail clippers or covering your child's hands with mittens to discourage scratching. Another hack is to gently smack the itchy area. It sounds strange but will satiate the itch while reducing the amount of damage done by fingernails raking against inflamed flesh.

Try to distract your toddler with snacks, toys they enjoy, and even a TV program they prefer. For the short-term, this kind of television exposure is the better alternative to a scratched skin rash where the laceration caused by friction and scratching could become infected. Do what you can to keep your little one safe even if you need to break your own rules on rare occasions to do so.

Gently Breaking Bad Habits

Fingernail-biting and thumb-sucking can become more problematic than being a social annoyance. Fingernails can become infected when germs enter the tiny cuts in torn fingertips. Also problematic is that thumb-sucking and excessive pacifier use beyond the first year can cause dental issues that will likely need to be corrected with braces and retainers in your child's preteen years, as their adult teeth become situated in their permanent positions within the mouth.

One way to curb the need to suck on thumbs or fingers is to place Band-Aids on the digits in question. Putting bitter substances or fingernail polish on fingernails might help in the short term, but it could also lead to a tolerance for chewing these potentially toxic deterrents. It would be swapping one vice for another.

Something else to consider if your child mouths or chews on objects that are non-food-related like plastic toys, dirt, or other non-food items is to offer foods that satisfy the texture they're craving. For a child who likes dirt, substitute cooked peas. Frozen peas will also provide the texture input they are seeking as the peas pop in their mouth. Canned peas are more squishy and may not satisfy your child's sensory needs, as well as the frozen kind when cooked.

Other substitutions include sliced cucumbers for a child who seeks crunch, cooked pasta if your little one tries to eat paper, and fruit-like sliced apples for a child who tries to chew on paint chips or ice. Whatever you notice your child chewing that isn't food needs to be removed from the mouth, and your child's hands need to be washed afterward because found items carry germs that cause gastrointestinal or upper respiratory illness and could also contain unsafe levels of lead that can negatively impact your child's development.

If a simple reminder to remove the item from their mouth is not enough to deter the most avid chewer, there may be an underlying health reason your child is seeking sustenance from non-food objects. These can include anemia, Pica, or a sensory concern. Your child may also be bored or hungry so be sure to keep this in mind to try before you rush to the doctor. If the problem persists, you will want to seek professional healthcare input if you feel like your child is actively eating non-food items instead of the normal developmental need to explore objects orally as most babies do until they are able to manipulate those same objects more adeptly in their hands.

If you ever suspect that your child has ingested chemicals, toxins, or medications, you should always call Poison Control —1-800-222-1222—for assistance in handling the situation. Their instructions vary depending upon what kind of substance your child has been exposed to, so keep the agency's phone number handy by keeping the phone number on your refrigerator or in the contacts in your phone so that you don't have to waste time searching for their phone number when you need help the most.

Traveling, Rather than Vacationing

It's one of life's many pleasures to explore the wonders planet Earth provides. To share those experiences with your child enriches their breadth of knowledge and offers boundless opportunities to bond. But traveling with a toddler can be challenging. Even just a trip to the local park can mean packing up a diaper bag for boo-boos and blowouts.

Diaper bags are great for storing snacks, diaper changing necessities like wipes and an extra set of clothes, and a first aid kit. Some designs are more cumbersome to carry. Toting along a purse and a diaper bag with your toddler in tow is impossible. You may opt to carry a larger backpack for your child's items; your wallet, phone, and keys can also go into the luxury storage inner pockets of a larger bag. One bag for two!

Pick a style and design that appeals to you and fits your needs. It will save you time packing only one bag, and you can keep your hands free to handle your little one.

Planning

You'll want to choose vacation destinations that are appropriate for your family situation. If your child is more mature, you will have fewer meltdowns to handle in less-than-kid-friendly places like museums, movie theaters, upscale resorts, and tourist attractions that carry an element of danger such as Hawai'i's Volcanoes National Park or the Grand Canyon.

Keep your little one safe and entertained by bringing along their electronics, toys, books, coloring instruments, and plenty of blank pages for their artwork. Pick a place to vacation that is appealing to your child, too. Disney World has several rides even a small child can enjoy, but the tickets are expensive, and the weather can be very challenging for you and your toddler. Bring a refillable water bottle for each member in your travel party. Each concession stand that serves cold beverages is legally required to supply their guests with a cup of ice water upon request. Feel free to ask a customer service member for enough ice water to fill up your water bottles.

You can also pack snacks and juice boxes for your child if they fit inside a small enough cooler for most attractions, zoos, and parks you can visit. Plan to take plenty of breaks (for restroom needs, to eat, and to rest). Little feet tire quickly; carrying a backpack of supplies and your child will tire you out, too. Even pushing a stroller takes its toll in summer weather.

If you try to fit too many experiences, attractions, or destinations in a single day, prepare for meltdowns. Try to meet your child's crying with your calm. Speak with care, using a tone to soothe their frustrations, and take deep breaths. Their stamina is much lower than an adult, so children require more frequent breaks and a heaping helping of understanding.

Plan your travel days and vacation stays around what you know your child is capable of and what you can handle as you manage the wonderful myriad of chaotic surprises raising a child can bring. You can only plan to a point but try to plan for every contingency you can imagine so you can get ahead of any tantrums before they manifest.

Packing

Plan on packing for every day you are away, plus three days-worth of clothes to change for accidents and messy days. Use an overnight bag if you are driving for an extended period of time. This way, you don't need to lug everything in and out just to stay the night somewhere you will be departing from in the morning. A change of clothes for the next day, a set of pajamas each, and a separate plastic container or tub with lid for toiletries is what you'll need to make a short hotel stay more manageable.

For your main luggage bag, you can fold an entire outfit up, wrapped inside the shirt or pants for the outfit. This method of folding provides more room for storage for several outfits for each family member.

Bring medications and syringes or cups that come with these medications in case your child runs a fever or has diarrhea. You'll want to pack light but be ready for any contingency that might occur. It's the best way to ensure a diaper blowout doesn't ruin a memorable family vacation.

Something to include for rainy days, or if your child seems bored during down times when everyone needs to rest, is to bring new toys or writing items that were bought on clearance well before the trip occurred and were set aside for this purpose. Your child will enjoy the novelty of having a new toy and you can enjoy a few moments of uninterrupted peace while you all make the most of your family time together.

We've included a packing list of all the essential items to ensure you have everything you could possibly need while not having to cart around the heaviest items:

- Enough clothing for each member of your family for as many days as you'll be on vacation, plus three extra outfits each
- Pajamas
- A light jacket for each member of your family
- Laundry bag for dirty clothes or garbage bags
- Diapers and wipes (bring a big enough box of each if you're traveling in your own vehicle, otherwise, bring enough to get you where you're going, and buy more when you arrive)
- Diaper ointment or rash cream
- Lotion
- Swim diapers
- A sun hat for your baby
- Bathing suit and towel
- Beach toys
- Sunglasses
- Sunscreen, insect repellant (be sure to check that both are safe to apply to baby)
- Aloe vera; sunburn-healing gel
- A change of shoes
- A portable crib (like a Pack-n-Play)
- Stroller and car seat
- Travel toys and comfort items for your child
- Chargers for any electronics you wish to bring along
- Refillable water bottles for each member of your family

- A purse or carry on with your wallet, ID, cell phone, charging cable, and keys
- Hairbrush or comb
- First aid kit (Band-Aids, antibiotic ointment, alcohol pads or wipes, plastic bag, medications, Tylenol or ibuprofen, Tums or other antacid, Benadryl or other antihistamine, thermometer, child or infant Tylenol, and saline)
- Toiletries, such as a toothbrush, toothpaste, pads or tampons, shampoo, body wash, conditioner, razor, shaving cream, and other products you and your family use. Store these upright in a clear tub with a lid if you're driving so that everyone has what they need, and the liquids won't spill in transit. Otherwise, you will benefit from sticking to carrying a toothbrush, toothpaste, and sanitary items with you and buying what you need once you arrive at your destination if you're traveling on a larger vessel with others where you cannot carry on liquid items.
- Umbrella, poncho, or coat if the weather requires it
- Snacks, bottles and sippy cups, a baby blanket, hand sanitizer, diapers, wipes, and a changing pad should be in your carry on or with you at all times
- Don't forget to pack snacks for yourself, too!

Anything you might need, you can always purchase once you arrive at your destination. So, don't stress, and bring only the essentials from the list that are appropriate for your family and situation.

Planes, Trains, and Automobiles

You don't want to be "that parent" whose kid won't stop crying or kicking the back of some stranger's seat, but in all reality, you might be, and that's okay. Whether others want to admit it or not, they were all once babies too who also needed to learn how to behave over the course of their childhood. No one comes into the world pre-programed with behaviors of which most adults approve. It all takes time and patience.

One way to abate your toddler's tantrums in confined spaces is to keep their minds and hands occupied. Offering multiple "happy snacks," drinks, small toys, coloring supplies like crayons and paper, and even an electronic device they can watch a movie on will help alleviate any opportunity for misbehavior. Get up and move with your child to explore their area if you can. Stretch your legs, too.

Understand that everything that is new to your child is an opportunity for growth and learning. They might be frightened by what they don't understand about sitting still or using an indoor voice, but the more they are exposed to these experiences, the better they will behave. With more practice going to various places, the more your child will understand about the world around them and how they fit into the flow of things.

Take frequent breaks if you're driving long-distance in the car. Using a tear-free book (that is a book with special pages that are rip-resistant) and inventing road games and songs (like 'I Spy' or using the alphabet to identify letters on signs and license plates or colors of objects like trees and orange construction barrels) will keep your child's attention. No matter where you go, always bring along a drink and something they can eat so that hunger doesn't complicate these travel situations.

If you or your child suffers from motion sickness, you could take a medication like Dramamine or an antihistamine like Benadryl. Herbal solutions include chewing a peppermint candy or sniffing certain essential oil fragrances like ginger, mint, or lavender. You can also infuse your child's stuffed animal or favorite blanket with these scents by putting a dryer sheet of the scent listed above in the dryer with the item that will accompany your child as you travel. Adding a few drops of mint or lavender essential oil (or sewing a sachet of dried lavender or mint herbs into the stuffed animal) will provide some comfort for your child, too.

If your child is developmentally able to safely chew hard candies or a lollipop, these are also useful in staving off motion sickness. Stay hydrated. Fill a reusable water bottle with ice water for you and your little one so that your body stays less susceptible to nausea. Always bring a plastic bag of some kind big enough to hold for your child in case they need to vomit. This way, it's less messy and the bag can be tied off for discreet handling of the sickness situation so it affects other passengers less.

Your child's needs come before anything that appeases other passengers, of course. You are their #1 advocate, their voice when they are unable to speak up for themselves. However, it is always going to be a more pleasant ride for everyone involved if you try to be polite and considerate of others, the same as you would expect them to be considerate of you and your child.

Ways to Maintain Your Sanity While Parenting a Toddler with an Attitude

Your little darling has developed a boisterous personality and you're not quite sure who they got their attitude from, but it's wreaking havoc with your plans, and your sanity. Trying to stay calm when you want to unleash the papa bear is hard, but you can do it! Maintain control of the situation by controlling your frustration. When you feel your temper flare, your heart rate increase, and your body tense, unclench your fists. Release the tension in your body one muscle group at a time and take slow, deep breaths as you do this.

Speak to your child in a firm, but calm, voice. An outburst of anger might scare them, and they will end up ignoring your instructions because all they will notice is the loudness of your voice. As you react in fear when you hear a loud sound and are faced with an immediate threat, your child's tiny body reacts the same way. They freeze, their eyes widen, and their nervous system turns on high alert to prepare them for the instinctual fight or flight response.

Instead of trying to yell at them into doing what needs to be done, calmly take their hand to guide them where they need to go or to what they need to do. When you lower your voice, their little ears must focus more to hear what you're saying. This method ensures you have their full attention to get the most out of your instructions.

Potty Training and Beyond

It's the moment most parents wait for as a momentous milestone of college graduation proportion: Potty training. Most toddlers are ready to begin toilet training between the ages of 18-24 months, with some children learning later or earlier (*9 tips for potty training your child in a week*, 2023). Every child develops at their own pace.

The best way to go about toilet training your child is to set your expectations low and prepare for accidents. You'll need to bring along a complete extra set of clothes (socks included), a plastic bag, and tons of wipes. Stay calm when accidents happen because anything that is shaming or angry will cause a setback in progress for your child. Their comfort level will diminish if they feel like they're doing something wrong. So, be patient and understanding. It's often a long, messy process.

You will notice when your child is ready to toilet train when they become more aware of their body. If their diaper is dry overnight, encourage your toddler to sit on a small potty chair or toilet insert that is appropriate for their size. Allow your little one to sit as long as they need to recognize the sensation of going to the bathroom.

They will use this feeling later to help them identify the feeling of needing to go to the restroom *before* they start to go.

Consistency is key. It is okay to have your child sit on a training potty in front of the TV during their favorite show for up to half an hour, each hour, to encourage them to use the potty. Keep snacks, a sippy cup, and a few toys or books nearby for your child to use as they learn. Once your child has successfully used the potty, praise their efforts. Go over the top with an excited tone and handclapping. Offer a reward like a sticker on a sticker chart, a toy from a prize box, or a piece of candy to encourage your child to want to use the potty again.

Wipe, and dress your child when they are finished so they can go about their day in cloth underwear. Encourage hand-washing with soap and warm water after every bathroom attempt. If your child has an accident, the sensation of wetness will discourage them from allowing an accident to happen in the future, but they also associate the sensation of having to go to the bathroom with what happens when they do "go." Their wet or soiled clothes will remind them how to prevent their clothes being soiled, and they will want to use the toilet instead. It takes time and consistent repetition to help your child become more aware of their body enough that they recognize the feeling of needing to go before it's too late.

When you consistently have your child sit on the toilet or potty chair before they are able to have an accident in their clothes, it helps them identify the sensations "before they need to go," "when they are going," and how relieved they feel once they've gone to the potty.

Look for signs that your child needs to use the toilet such as holding themselves, passing gas, or shifting their weight from one foot to the other in a kind of "potty dance." Also, if you realize your child hasn't peed or pooped within the last hour, it would be well-advised to set aside time for them to sit on the toilet so they can "take care of business." You may also find that setting a "potty watch" or timer for every hour is a helpful reminder until your child starts to go to the toilet themselves or letting you know when they need to go, independently.

A word of advice for all children: Onesies are adorable for infants and crawlers, but once your child begins to toddle around, opt for separate pieces like a t-shirt and pants or a dress with shorts underneath. Overalls, bodysuits, and rompers make toilet training incredibly complicated, if not impossible. Separates are optimal for this time of transition. Also, choose snaps or pull-up pants instead of buttons or zippers until your child is more proficient in using the toilet on their own.

Tips for Training Girls

Girls should always learn to wipe from front to back to avoid fecal contamination that leads to urinary tract infections. This can be a difficult concept at first, so you may need to help your little one by wiping them at the beginning. Next, you will encourage them to wipe themselves giving helpful advice if they need more help.

Tips for Training Boys

You have unlocked a new use for Cheerios or other O-shaped cereals: Target practice. Sprinkle about five Cheerios into the toilet to teach your little boy to aim while standing to urinate. One caveat with teaching boys to potty on the toilet is that they need to sit to defecate and stand to urinate. Begin with the basics by having your child sit for both.

Then, make it an exciting game to aim for each "target" as they pee in the toilet. You may need to invest in a step-stool so that they can reach the toilet with less of a mess if they miss.

Clean the bathroom and toilet with bleach to kill the strong odor urine leaves behind.

Afterword

Parenting is undoubtedly one of the most challenging and rewarding experiences a person can have. From dealing with sleepless nights to navigating the complexities of discipline and balancing work and family life, it can often feel like an overwhelming task. However, with the right mindset, tools, and techniques, navigating parenthood can become an enjoyable and fulfilling experience. The advice provided in *Baby Hacks* is designed to equip parents with the necessary skills to navigate the difficulties of parenting with confidence. From setting realistic expectations and building a support network to prioritizing self-care and using positive reinforcement techniques, the strategies outlined in this book have been proven effective in helping parents overcome the challenges of raising children.

One of the key takeaways from this book is the importance of understanding that there is no one-size-fits-all approach to parenting. Every child is unique, and as such, requires a tailored approach to their upbringing. However, by following the principles outlined in this book, parents can develop the flexibility and adaptability necessary to meet the needs of their children and navigate the various stages of their development. Ultimately, parenting is a journey full of ups and downs, but with the right mindset, knowledge, and support, it is a journey that can be successfully navigated. By implementing the advice in this book, parents can feel confident in their abilities to raise happy, healthy, and well-adjusted children. So, take a deep breath, trust in yourself, and let this book be your guide on this wonderful and rewarding journey of parenthood.

Preparing for a newborn baby can seem like a daunting task, but with the right approach and mindset, it can actually be an enjoyable and fulfilling experience. By understanding what your baby needs and preparing accordingly, you can ensure that you are fully equipped to provide them with the love, care, and attention they require. You now know that the first step in preparing for a baby is to gain a clear understanding of their needs. Because you know to focus on these core needs, you are adequately prepared to care for your little one. You are also in the know about preparing a comfortable and safe environment for them. You are aware that the nursery has to be warm, cozy, and free of any potential hazards. In addition to creating a safe and comfortable environment, you have also stocked up on the necessary supplies for your baby. By having these essentials on hand, you can readily parent knowing that your baby's basic needs are always met.

Having a strong support system can help alleviate some of the stress and anxiety that can come with caring for a newborn and you know what steps to take in order to build one. Remember that preparing for a baby is a process that takes time and patience. Don't be afraid to take things one step at a time and seek out help and support when needed. By focusing on the essentials, creating a safe and comfortable environment, and seeking out support, you can prepare for your baby with confidence and ease. Preparing for a baby may seem overwhelming, but with the right approach, it can be a straightforward and enjoyable process. So, take a deep breath, trust in yourself, and enjoy the journey of preparing for your new bundle of joy.

Leave a Review

Reviews provide a way for parents to narrow down their options and make more informed decisions. Other parents who have used the product can offer insights into its practicality and effectiveness. New parents want to ensure they are purchasing products that are safe and reliable for their babies, and reviews can provide valuable information on these aspects. They can help new parents save time and money. With so many baby-related products available, it can be tempting to purchase the first thing that catches your eye. However, reviews can offer an indication of whether a product is worth the investment or not, helping parents avoid wasting money on items that may not be useful in the long run.

Without even intending it, reviews offer a sense of community and support for new parents. Seeing positive reviews from other parents can help build confidence in decision-making, while negative reviews can serve as a warning to avoid certain products. Overall, reviews provide a valuable resource for new parents who want to make informed decisions and ensure the safety and wellbeing of their babies.

After reading *Baby Hacks*, please consider leaving a review on Amazon and Goodreads. Your review can help others discover this book and make a more informed decision before purchasing it. Reviews play a crucial role in helping me reach new readers and gain visibility on Amazon's platform. When a book has more positive reviews, it appears higher in search results and is more likely to catch a potential reader's attention. Your review doesn't have to be long or detailed; even a short sentence or two can make a difference.

It can be as simple as sharing what you enjoyed about the book or why you would recommend it to others. You can choose to rate the book with a star rating and add a written review. Your feedback matters and can help grow readership. So, please take a few moments to share your thoughts and leave a review. Thank you for your support and for helping other readers find their next great resource in their parenting journey.

Where To Find More Information

Books and Websites

If you ever need to find additional information about a specific topic, you may need to look beyond this book. The following are some recommended books and websites for new dads that offer practical hacks, information, and tips.

Books

1. *Parenting with Love and Logic* by Foster Cline and Jim Fay
2. *The Whole-Brain Child: 12 Revolutionary Strategies to Nurture Your Child's Developing Mind* by Daniel J. Siegel and Tina Payne Bryson
3. *How to Talk So Kids Will Listen & Listen So Kids Will Talk* by Adele Faber and Elaine Mazlish
4. *Simplicity Parenting: Using the Extra*ordinary Power of Less to Raise Calmer, Happier, and More Secure Kids by Kim John Payne and Lisa M. Ross

5. *No-Drama Discipline: The Whole-Brain Way to Calm the Chaos and Nurture Your Child's Developing Mind* by Daniel J. Siegel and Tina Payne Bryson

Websites

- Parenting Science: On this website, you will encounter evidence-based articles, especially on a variety of topics relating to parenting. This includes development stages, discipline techniques, sleep schedules, and nutrition.
- Zero to Three: This website is concerned with topics about the development of infants and toddlers between the ages of zero and three. The information is targeted to support parents and caregivers.
- The Gottman Institute: A parent can expect to find research-based information on how to strengthen their relationship with their children, including tips on various parenting styles and communication techniques.
- Common Sense Media: On this site, a parent will find information about media platforms and if they are age-appropriate for their children. There are reviews on movies, TV shows, apps, and video games.
- HealthyChildren.org: The American Academy of Pediatrics created this website to provide parents with relevant and updated information about pediatric health. The topic revolves around development topics, as well as information about your child's nutrition, sleep, and safety.

The abovementioned books and websites could add value in your quest for more information during your parenting journey. It is always important to remember that your child is unique and different. What works for your neighbor or your friend's child might not work for yours and vice versa. You never know which piece of advice will work, so always be open to advice and support from your family members and friends as well as health care providers and community workers.

Professional Organizations

Coming together and meeting under a professional organization or support group can provide help accessing various resources and information related to parenting. This can also give you a sense of community and belonging as a parent. Within these professional organizations, you will feel as if you are in a safe space in order to connect with those who are in a similar position as you or who are experiencing the same challenges. These professional organizations also often provide access to experts in the field who are open to providing specialized knowledge about parenting.

By using the resources from professional organizations, you will feel more confident to get through the challenges related to raising your baby from infant to toddler stage and even beyond. As a parent, you will have to know how to navigate the healthcare, education, and social service systems. You may not know what each of these systems do or where their limits are. Always remember that you are not alone. You will be able to know who to call on for help by getting the information from the professional organizations. By joining the communities created by these professional organizations, you will associate with others who can support you during the specific challenge you may be encountering. You can gain so much insight by sharing with parents who are going through, or have gone through, what you are experiencing.

Where To Find More Information

There is no specific class that you can attend that will show you exactly how to parent. Having a baby is like living in the wild, wild west; you have no idea what will happen. Due to this unpredictable nature of parenting, you might need a source of educational material on various aspects of child-rearing. There are some professional organizations that can train and teach you on topics surrounding parenting, advocacy and child development. By attending the courses or reading through their educational material, you can gain some useful information and boost your confidence in your parenting skills.

Find below various recommended professional organizations where you can find useful resources during your parenting journey.

- National Parenting Education Network (NPEN) is a non-profit organization where you can get educational material to share with parents during sessions that provide resources and support.
- National Alliance on Mental Illness (NAMI) is also a non-profit organization that provides support for people who may have mental illnesses or are affected by them. They provide a community for families who have to deal with mental illness.
- Parents Anonymous provides a platform for parents to take parenting lessons and join together in support groups to offer emotional support and practical advice and advocacy efforts for parents and caregivers.
- Association for Middle Level Education (AMLE): AMLE is a professional organization that focuses on the education and development of middle school students. They offer resources and support for parents, educators, and professionals.

- Autism Society: The Autism Society is a non-profit organization that provides advocacy, education, and support for individuals and families affected by autism.

These are just a few examples of the many professional organizations and support groups available to you. It's important to find the organization or group that suits your needs and the issues you are facing as a parent.

Connecting with other parents and finding resources and support can be incredibly beneficial for a number of reasons. It can be comforting and validating to connect with other parents who are experiencing similar challenges. This can help reduce your feelings of isolation and provide a sense of community. Other parents can offer valuable advice and support based on their own experiences. This can help parents navigate challenges and make informed decisions. Hearing how others navigated the same issue can provide access to a wide range of resources, including books, articles, websites, support groups, and professional organizations.

Networking with other parents for support can help improve mental health by reducing stress, anxiety, and feelings of isolation. Accessing resources and support can help parents develop skills and knowledge that can improve their parenting and advocacy efforts. You can become more effective advocates for your children, whether it's in the school system, the healthcare system, or other areas. It's important for you to seek out the resources and support that best meet your needs and to take advantage of the resources available to you.

Online Communities and Support Groups

Online communities and support groups for parents offer several benefits, including providing a safe space for parents to share their experiences, challenges, and concerns with other parents who are going through similar situations. These communities offer a sense of belonging and provide emotional support to parents. They offer a wealth of information and resources on various topics related to parenting, including child development, discipline, and health. You can learn from the experiences of others and access resources that may not be available in your local area. Online support groups offer the convenience of being available 24/7, allowing parents to access information and support whenever they need it, regardless of their location or schedule.

Here are some recommended online communities and support groups for you to explore.

- BabyCenter Community: A popular online community with forums for pregnancy, parenting, and trying to conceive.
- What to Expect Community: A community for parents with forums for pregnancy, baby, and toddler stages.
- Single Parents Network: A support group for single parents offering resources, forums, and chat rooms.
- Parents Without Partners: A non-profit organization providing support and social opportunities for single parents.
- MomsRising: A grassroots organization advocating for policies to support mothers and families. They offer resources, blogs, and opportunities to take action on issues affecting parents.

Where To Find More Information

- La Leche League International: A support group for breastfeeding mothers offering information, resources, and local group meetings.
- National Association of Parents: An organization providing resources and support for parents of children with special needs.
- Postpartum Support International: A support group for mothers experiencing perinatal mood and anxiety disorders.
- The Dad Network: A support group for fathers offering resources, forums, and social opportunities.
- Circle of Moms: A community for mothers offering forums on various parenting topics, including adoption, special needs, and pregnancy.

Use search engines or social media platforms to find online communities and support groups that cater to your interests, parenting style, or specific needs. You can also ask for recommendations from friends or family members. Once you've joined an online community or support group, take the initiative to participate in discussions. Ask questions, share your experiences, and provide support to other members. Be open to different parenting styles and perspectives. You may encounter parents who have different approaches to parenting but remember that everyone's journey is unique.

Remember that online communities and support groups are often private spaces. Respect the privacy of other members and avoid sharing their personal information or experiences without their consent. Many online communities and support groups offer numerous resources, including articles, videos, and podcasts. Take advantage of these resources to learn more about parenting topics that interest you. They also often host virtual events, such as webinars, conferences, or meetups.

Where To Find More Information

Attend these events to connect with other parents, learn from experts, and engage with the community.

Consider paid services, such as coaching, counseling, or courses, especially if you feel like you need more personalized support. Remember, finding the right online community or support group may take time, but the benefits can be significant. By connecting with other parents online, you can find a community of people who understand the challenges of parenthood like no one else in your real life does.

Bibliography

Balasundaram, P. and Avulakunta, I. D. (2023, March 8). *Human growth and development*. National Library of Medicine. https://www.ncbi.nlm.nih.gov/books/NBK567767

Ballard, L. (2023, March 22). *Is potty training easier for girls or boys?*. Kimberly-Clark. https://www.pull-ups.com/en-us/resources/tips-advice/potty-training-girls/easier-or-harder-than-boys.

Bernard-Bonnin, A. (2006, October). *Feeding problems of infants and toddlers*. National Library of Medicine. https://pubmed.ncbi.nlm.nih.gov/17279184/

The Best Family. (2023, March 31). *Is your mini human always breaking crayons?*. Facebook [video]. https://www.facebook.com/reel/524553086531485/?s=single_unit

Black, T. (2021, December 15). *Homemade natural baby shampoo and wash*. Don't Mess With Mama. https://dontmesswithmama.com/natural-homemade-baby-wash-and-shampoo/

Breastfeeding. (2023). World Health Organization. https://www.who.int/health-topics/breastfeeding#tab=tab_1

Child development (1)- newborn to three months. (2021). Victoria State Government. https://www.betterhealth.vic.gov.au/health/healthyliving/child-development-1-newborn-to-three-months

Child health (0-6). (2022, February 23). Victoria State Government. https://www.betterhealth.vic.gov.au/healthyliving/child-health-0-6

Colic. (2023). Johns Hopkins Medicine. https://www.hopkinsmedicine.org/health/conditions-and-diseases/colic

Dessinger, H. (2023). *How to make tallow balm*. Mommypotamus. https://mommypotamus.com/how-to-make-tallow-balm

Dessinger, H. (2023). 7 causes of diaper rash and how to treat them naturally. Mommypotamus. https://mommypotamus.com/7-causes-of-diaper-rash-and-how-to-treat-them-naturally

Dessinger, H. (2023). *Which essential oils are safe for kids? 70+ oils & how to use them*. Mommypotamus. https://mommypotamus.com/safe-essential-oils-babies-children

Durbin, D. R. and Hoffman, B. D. (2018, August 30). *Child passenger safety*. National Library of Medicine. https://pubmed.ncbi.nlm.nih.gov/30166368

Bibliography

Fabian-Weber, N. (2021, November 5). *How to get kids to leave when they're having fun (without a meltdown)*. Care. https://www.care.com/c/how-to-get-kids-to-leave-without-tantrum-when-having-fun

Gammons, K. H. [@kaseyhgammons]. (2022, August 13). *What is the 50/30/20 budgeting strategy? #budgeting #financialliteracy #financialeducation #budget* [Video]. TikTok. https://www.tiktok.com/@kaseyhgammons/video/7131544599901900074

Hack. (2023). Merriam-Webster Dictionary. https://www.merriam-webster.com/dictionary/hack

Heid, M. (2016, May 25). *5 parenting hacks for new dads that you won't find in baby books*. Men's Health. https://www.menshealth.com/trending-news/a19521477/easy-parenting-hacks/

Horn, S. R. and Feder, A. (2018, January 31). *Understanding resilience and preventing and treating PTSD*. Department of Psychology University of Oregon. https://www.frames.gov/documents/nafri/SFA.3_Understanding_Resilience_and_Preventing_and.6.pdf

Hovis, T. (2023). *Pica in toddlers and preschoolers*. SuperKids Nutrition. https://www.superkidsnutrition.com/pica-in-toddlers-and-preschoolers

How long does it take to have an allergic reaction to a bee sting?. (2021, January 29). Oak Brook Allergists. https://www.oakbrookallergists.com/2021/01/29/how-long-does-it-take-to-have-an-allergic-reaction-to-a-bee-sting

Kate. (2012, February 27). *DIY: Teething cream*. Modern Alternative Mama. https://modernalternativemama.com/2012/2/27/monday-health-wellness-homemade-teething-cream/#.VBha7_mSwkQ

Kutner, L. (2016, May 17). *How children develop empathy*. PsychCentral. https://psychcentral.com/lib/how-children-develop-empathy#1

Laura. (2023). *Travel packing lists for mom, baby, and toddler*. The Organized Mom Life. https://theorganizedmomlife.com/pack

Motion Sickness. (2021, January 18). Cleveland Clinic. https://my.clevelandclinic.org/health/articles/12782-motion-sickness

9 tips for potty training your child in a week. (2023, April 24). World Humanitarian Movement. https://wohum.org/9-tips-for-potty-training-your-child-in-a-week

Parents Editors. (2015, July 2). *When can I stop using baby soap?*. Parents Magazine. https://www.parents.com/baby/new-parent/when-can-i-stop-using-baby-soap

Poison ivy, oak, and sumac: How to treat the rash. (2023). American Academy of Dermatology Association. https://www.aad.org/public/everyday-care/itchy-skin/poison-ivy/treat-rash

Bibliography

Rooting reflex definition. (2023). HarperCollins Publishers. https://www.-collinsdictionary.com/us/dictionary/english/rooting-reflex

Shaw, G. (2009). *Baby's first year: How infants develop*. WebMD. https://www.webmd.com/parenting/baby/features/stages-of-development

White noise. (2023). Merriam-Webster Dictionary. https://www.merriam-webster.com/dictionary/white%20noise#

Made in the USA
Las Vegas, NV
19 December 2023

83119105R00080